# Critical
# Conditions

# Critical Conditions

## Addressing Education Emergencies Through Integrated Student Supports

ELAINE WEISS
BRUCE LEVINE
KIMBERLY STERIN

Harvard Education Press
Cambridge, Massachusetts

Paperback ISBN 9781682539163

Library of Congress Cataloging-in-Publication Data

Names: Weiss, Elaine (Writer on education policy), author. | Levine, Bruce
    (Clinical professor), author. | Sterin, Kimberly, author.
Title: Critical conditions : addressing education emergencies through
    integrated student supports / Elaine Weiss, Bruce Levine, Kimberly
    Sterin.
Description: Cambridge, Massachusetts : Harvard Education Press, [2024] |
    Includes bibliographical references and index.
Identifiers: LCCN 2024016085 | ISBN 9781682539163 (paperback)
Subjects: LCSH: Student assistance programs—United States—Case studies. |
    Crisis management—United States—Case studies. | COVID-19 Pandemic,
    2020—Social aspects—United States—Case studies. | Community and
    school—United States—Case studies.
Classification: LCC LB3430.5 .W45 2024 | DDC 371.7—dc23/eng/20240709
LC record available at https://lccn.loc.gov/2024016085

Published by Harvard Education Press,
an imprint of the Harvard Education Publishing Group

Harvard Education Press
8 Story Street
Cambridge, MA 02138

Cover Design: Jackie Shepherd Design
Cover Images: Inside Creative House via Shutterstock; RikoBest via Shutterstock

The typefaces in this book are Carrara and Gotham.

*To all the dedicated people who work with
and within schools, even and especially during crises,
who are on the front lines for the rest of us every day*

# CONTENTS

# FOREWORD

EXPERIENCE CAN BE A CRUEL TEACHER. For leaders, this universal truth is most notably applicable to crises. Unfortunately, there are no textbooks, CliffsNotes, YouTube videos, or cheat sheets to help us pass the unexpected "pop quiz" of crisis leadership.

My leadership pop quiz began on May 22, 2011, at 5:41 p.m. in Joplin, Missouri. That is when the costliest tornado in US history took the lives of 161 of our friends and neighbors, including seven of my students and a school secretary. Punctuating the cruel nature of that experience was the fact that we had just finished celebrating the many accomplishments of the Class of 2011. In addition to the horrific loss of life, ten of our buildings—nine schools and our central office—were damaged or destroyed.

One of the many blessings I have experienced since that fateful day is the opportunity to walk alongside school and community leaders following some of the nation's most horrific disasters over the last dozen years. Hurricanes Harvey, Maria, and Michael. Superstorm Sandy. Tornadoes in Moore, Oklahoma, Wynne, Arkansas, and Rolling Fork, Mississippi. Wildfires in Paradise, California, and Lahaina, Maui. Flooding in Humphreys County, Tennessee. And then, of course, our shared COVID-19 pandemic experience. Indeed, experience is a cruel teacher.

As I travel the country presenting lessons learned to help respond to the latest crisis, the first question I typically get asked is, "What matters most?" or "What is that one thing that makes a difference?" My response is always the same: "Relationships matter." The relationship between local human-service agencies and the schools matters. The relationship between the faith-based community and the schools matters. The relationship between business/industry and the schools matters. The relationship between families and the schools matters. Those relationships assist leaders in preparing for, responding to, and recovering from the unthinkable. In short, relationships don't just matter; they carry the day.

The follow-up question I often get asked is, "How do we know when those local relationships are in a good place?" My answer is equally simple: "When you know how your community partners 'take their coffee'... one lump or two?" The point is that community leaders need to know one another personally. Knowing how each other thinks, respecting the content of each other's character, and understanding the heart that underpins the strategic response and recovery following a crisis is paramount to both the short-term response and long-term recovery effort.

I am blessed to have had the opportunity to work alongside the authors for nearly a decade. True to my advice above, I not only know how they take their coffee but also how they take their rice pudding—a dessert that became a tradition at working meetings. My first direct engagement with this trio was with Elaine. We were introduced and became fast friends. We were an unlikely duo, given the fact she was an infamous liberal Capital Beltway "insider" and I was from the conservative Midwestern buckle of the Bible Belt. Politics aside, we found our common ground quickly: kids, education, and community.

Then Elaine introduced me to Bruce, and we also became fast friends. We were jovial in our thoughts on life and work but serious and direct when it came to our conversations around public policy and community-based strategies with the potential to improve life outcomes for children, youth, and families. I have personally enjoyed every conversation I have had with Bruce. He breaks the mold of what one may think of someone with a law degree working in academia. Thoughtful, reflective, passionate, caring, and action-oriented are the immediate words that come to mind. And yes, he is also brilliant.

Kim is the newest member of my circle of friends and colleagues. As a former middle and high school English teacher, she brings so much to this work. Kim has "boots on the ground" experience working with adolescents in high-poverty schools. And, like so many caring educators across the country, she took it upon herself to meet the basic needs of her students in the absence of available resources. She understands that Maslow comes before Bloom, or, as a minister in Fairbanks, Alaska, shared with me many years ago, "An empty stomach has no ears." And, yes, I know how she feels about rice pudding. It turns out she is not a fan and prefers salty snacks.

Bruce, Elaine, and Kim are more than just authors of a great book on a relevant national topic in our nation's schools and communities. They are a team. And like any championship-caliber team, they are laser-focused on a singular goal. In their case, that goal is to develop local integrated student supports (ISS) in communities across the country to change the life trajectory of our nation's most vulnerable children and families. They also understand that community engagement and the establishment of ISS is both an art and a science, combined with a bit of hip-hop. The point is that there are most definitely universal truths when it comes to community engagement. But there is also a little bit of improv and much creativity. It's very challenging, but it is worthwhile and much-needed work.

One of the early lessons I learned after our disaster in Joplin was that, for a moment, everyone directly impacted by that storm, regardless of social class, became vulnerable. Thousands had lost everything in thirty-two minutes. However, in the hours, days, weeks, and months that followed, those who struggled most to recover from the storm were our financially unstable and under-resourced families. It should have come as no surprise that most did not have renter's insurance. Most did not have another family member or a friend with a spare bedroom or two. Most did not have access to another form of transportation. And most had no financial resources tucked away in a "rainy day" fund.

What makes this book unique in the community engagement space is this team of authors' ability to make the case that ISS, previously defined and illustrated in their collective body of work, should be strongly considered as a local framework for communities' efforts to prepare for, respond to, and recover from a crisis. Between the covers of *Critical Conditions: Addressing Education Emergencies Through Integrated Student Supports*, their research, case studies, interviews, and stories of practitioner experiences bring this timely, relevant topic to life for school and community leaders. It is an opportunity to pause, reflect on the lessons we have learned during our shared pandemic experiences, and begin those conversations with leaders and policy makers over a cup of coffee or, perhaps, a fresh bowl of rice pudding. Enjoy.

—C. J. Huff
President of the C. J. Huff Group

# Introduction: Reframing the US Education System Post-Pandemic

SCHOOLS IN THE UNITED STATES have been operating under emergency conditions for years. Long before the acute, nationwide health emergency of the COVID-19 pandemic, many school communities were contending with intense and ongoing crises. As the compounding emergencies of economic instability, climate change, and mental health challenges have been impacting students, families, and community members, so have they impacted the classroom. In the Appalachian region of Kentucky, for example, almost no family, and no school community, has been left unscarred by the mass job losses and the opioid epidemic the area has been battling since the early 2000s. Similarly, families in North Minneapolis have been contending with chronic homelessness and gun violence, putting students and teachers in perpetual states of grief and trauma. Increasingly extreme weather conditions and sudden natural disasters have caused schools, especially in the South and West, to close down, pushing some districts to seek alternative modes of schooling.

As community institutions, schools bear witness to the scope and depth of these critical conditions—and also the weight of responsibility. When students are hungry, teachers notice. When students cannot afford school supplies, teachers notice. When students are depressed, teachers notice. Some students and families experience needs in areas such as employment, housing, and physical and mental health that are so urgent and dire that they impede students' ability to learn, develop, and achieve in the classroom. In some areas where these conditions have reached emergency levels, schools have not been able to proceed using the country's traditional approach to education.

As educators and educational leaders are often on the frontlines to help when their communities face such education emergencies, schools have also led the country in developing an approach to address them: integrated student supports (ISS). Usually using schools as a central hub for delivery, the ISS approach provides a network of supportive services to students and families so that they may have their baseline needs met and be better able to access education. We have found that school communities using the ISS approach have played a central role in supporting community resilience and economic stabilization, even through emergencies.

The COVID-19 pandemic introduced the US school system at large to the concept of providing "education in emergencies"—one that has long been well known in, but mostly limited to, countries dealing with war, drought, floods, and famine.[1] This framework emphasizes the importance of education in such crisis contexts and provides guidance on how educators can help compensate for the lack of stability and structure children are experiencing in other aspects of their lives.

While relatively little known among wealthier, Western education systems, "education in emergencies" has broad application for children, teachers, and schools in many regions of the world. For example, in a 2013 report, the international aid organization Save the Children estimated that fifty million school-aged children across the globe were at that time not in school due to conflicts in various violence-stricken regions.[2]

Another example is the effort to educate refugees from the conflicts in Syria and Afghanistan who are currently in camps in the Greek islands. Some education systems have almost halted at times when contending with such crises, while others have found ways to adapt in order to provide an educational outlet to students even during these emergencies.

A 2020 UNICEF Innocenti working paper provides a "rapid review" of these practices with the goal of informing education systems going into the COVID-19 pandemic.[3] The working paper draws on and provides a framework and guidance for education that takes place in crisis contexts, emphasizing the critical importance of schools as physically and emotionally safe spaces for children who are experiencing trauma. It speaks, also, to the need to structure schools to sustain academic instruction so as to maintain normalcy and continue learning, as well as to address students' traumas via various curricula and other physical and social-emotional supports.

So while many nations and their education systems have a history of contending with severe ongoing crisis, for better or worse, the United States has traditionally not been framed as being in such a state of emergency, and its education system as a whole had not been prepared to manage a wide-scale, long-term issue such as a pandemic. Then, in the spring of 2020, every student in the United States was simultaneously affected by an "emergency," and the sudden onset of emergency education became a reality as public and private schools across the country began closing down, state by state. By March 11, when a global pandemic had been declared by the World Health Organization, close to every school in the United States was shuttered.[4] Suddenly, nearly all fifty-five million K–12 students in the country were confined to their homes for the foreseeable future, and the more than thirteen thousand US school districts, plus the numerous charter and private school communities, had to make an immediate shift to a remote learning environment.

It is important to keep in mind that unlike many of our peer nations, the United States is home to *thousands* of education systems—with curriculum, policies, practices, and many other characteristics varying from one state to another, and within states by district. Further variation exists among school types, such as between traditional public schools, public charter schools, private schools, and religious schools. From the country's founding, the United States has viewed education as a community-driven institution and, accordingly, has given localities the highest degree of autonomy and control among the three levels of educational governance (federal, state, and local).[5] This highly decentralized nature of the US education system at large prohibited the nation's schools from taking a uniform approach to the challenges brought on by COVID-19. Some cite the lack of a nationwide educational response plan as a weakness and bemoan the lack of unity, as local education systems made differing and often conflicting decisions as the pandemic continued.[6] On the other hand, local autonomy in US education provided an environment for the many educational innovations that emerged during the crisis.[7]

As Emma García and Elaine Weiss describe in a paper for the Economic Policy Institute, stakeholders in our education communities were largely unprepared for the combination of challenges they faced with the sudden shift to online learning and forced "homeschooling" for millions of children.[8] The lack of preparedness led to deeply inadequate and inequitable access to online classes and disrupted learning, on top of often severe stress related to the need for basic necessities like food, housing, and health care.[9] The challenges the COVID-19 pandemic laid bare were exacerbated by many of the pre-existing structural inequities in the US education system at all levels and society at large.

Notwithstanding these differing impacts of COVID-19 across the country's many demographic groups and regions, children, parents, and teachers in every school community were experiencing a common crisis together in real time. That said, while the crisis caused by the arrival of COVID-19 was an "emergency" for our nation's schools by any definition, in reality, as we discuss in the next chapter, millions of children and thousands of their teachers in schools across the country were endeavoring to learn and teach in emergency contexts long before the pandemic. Over the past forty years, school communities have been contending with massive job displacement, substance abuse, increasing numbers of deaths of despair, gun violence, and climate change, among other phenomena. The resulting pressures on our social systems—due to increases in incarceration, parental absences, homelessness, and other social challenges—have been growing, and schools have been far from immune from them.

As a result, schools are increasingly operating not only as institutions of teaching and learning, but as nutritional support centers, social welfare agencies, mental health triage providers, and even surrogate parents and families. For example, for the decade since recovery from the Great Recession of 2008 was officially declared, over half of all public school students across the country qualified for free and reduced-price meals, meaning they lived in households that could not consistently feed them three solid meals a day without cutting back on rent, clothing, transportation, or other basics.[10] In states across the South, where poverty is the most intense, some districts have been serving student bodies that are virtually all poor, with poverty itself constituting a crisis. Highlighting the realities of this context even "before suffering the harshest effects of the Great Recession," Georgia writer and professor Steve Suitts analyzed data from a 2010 Southern Education Foundation report to document the extent of this problem:

> Twelve of the twenty-five school districts with the highest rates of extreme child poverty were in the South, including five districts in Texas and four in Mississippi. Fifty-six of the one hundred school districts with the highest rates throughout the nation were located in the South. At the same time, every state in the country has school districts with very high rates of extreme child poverty.... At least two out of every five southern school districts in the study had a rate of extreme child poverty of 10 percent or more.[11]

On the federal level, the policy makers who shape our public education system have scarcely acknowledged, let alone adapted to, this national reality, beyond rhetoric and occasional or marginal actions. This failure to take into account and address head-on the impacts of poverty is encapsulated in the federal No Child Left Behind (NCLB) Act, the 2002 reauthorization of the flagship Elementary and Secondary Education Act (ESEA). While never fully funded, ESEA, which was originally enacted as part of President Lyndon B. Johnson's War on Poverty, was intended to help high-poverty school districts compensate for inequitable and insufficient state and local funding. After decades of progress toward narrowing income- and race-based achievement gaps through this supports-based approach, however, the 1990s brought a shift toward using student achievement to "hold schools accountable." Indeed, in 2016, Suitts noted that "test-based accountability has been the law of the land for the past 30 years—which means that it is the only system that many educators have experienced."[12]

NCLB's narrow focus on standardized test scores as a means to both capture students' knowledge and abilities, and to assess teacher and school performance, not only ignored the crises described above, but in practice punished those who suffered from them. This is at the heart of a range of critiques compiled by former Vermont superintendent of the year, William Matthis, and former urban educator and education professor at the University of California, Berkeley, Tina M. Trujillo, in their 2016 book *Learning from the Federal Market-Based Reforms: Lessons for the Every Student Succeeds Act.*[13] Published in the wake of Congress's 2015 reauthorization of ESEA as the Every Student Succeeds Act (ESSA), the authors write in a commentary introducing the book,

> In a barren time for bi-partisan cooperation late in 2015, both Democrats and Republicans were happy to get rid of No Child Left Behind (NCLB). The K-12 education law was almost universally excoriated as being a failure—particularly in that most important goal of closing

the achievement gap. Looking at long-term trends from the National Assessment of Educational Progress, gains were seen in some areas but the achievement gap was stuck. NCLB provided no upward blips on the charts.[14]

Unfortunately, they note, ESSA does little to shift away from this approach that proved both unsuccessful and punitive, leaving most states—and thus the vast majority of school districts—to implement similar test-based regimes under the new federal law and to continue to ignore, or deny, the serious impacts of education emergencies schools face.

At the same time, both NCLB and ESSA did acknowledge the importance of attending to out-of-school needs in order to support in-school achievement, even if efforts to address them were not substantial enough to make broader impacts. The Comprehensive School Reform Demonstration, which was part of NCLB, aimed to apply a holistic strategy to improve both academic and nonacademic outcomes; however, its impact has rendered mixed results without indicating clear connections between strategies implemented and educational outcomes.[15] Some federal initiatives subsequently began to shift from top-down, accountability models to bottom-up, place-based strategies. These include Full-Service Community Schools (FSCS), which have been growing in popularity and are supported by increased federal and state-level investments nationwide.[16]

Despite these stalls and weaknesses in federal education strategies, our investigation of the K–12 education landscape suggests that there are a growing number of pockets of strength around the country. This book highlights a subset of districts and communities that have recognized the need to address the previously mentioned "emergencies" education stakeholders confront and that are doing things very differently—they employ ISS. Some of these districts are implementing federal- and state-supported place-based initiatives like FSCS and Promise Neighborhoods. Others have enacted locally driven models operating either as independent nonprofits or with the support of universities or other local institutions. All are part of networks, organizations, or initiatives that transcend any particular community, such as Bright Futures USA, City Connects, the EdRedesign Lab, or Communities In Schools, among others. And some are employing more than one of these concepts and models.

Whatever the exact language used, however, all have recognized the impacts of poverty, trauma, and various other social challenges—crises that we consider ongoing emergencies—on students and their families. These communities have undertaken the responsibility and recognized the need for schools, as de facto first responders to these realities, to take a proactive, supportive, whole-child approach to addressing and, as much as possible, alleviating and even preventing these problems that impede effective teaching and learning and limit what our schools can accomplish.[17]

In other words, these school communities had been operating, to some degree, under an "education in emergencies" context for many years before COVID-19 arrived. They had been feeding children who were hungry, clothing students who lacked sufficient and appropriate attire, providing mental health support and crisis intervention, and working with those children's families to address barriers to school readiness like joblessness and homelessness. As we reflected on our study of these schools, it stood to reason, then, that these communities entered the pandemic-induced lockdown better prepared than many of the nation's other schools to handle the sudden onslaught of changes, including the spikes in student, family, and community needs that the pandemic produced.

By looking at the experience of schools in ISS communities during the pandemic, we saw the opportunity to assess the degree to which the ISS model might hold promise for enabling our schools to continue to operate (and do so more effectively) in the face of the growing reality of the United States contending with "education emergencies" on an ongoing basis. This book draws on over a year of interviews with a variety of stakeholders in multiple, very different ISS communities across the country, along with extensive research on both the theory of ISS and its practical implications.

## OVERVIEW OF THE BOOK

The first chapter delves into the reality and extent of education emergencies in the United States. Given the extensive research that has been done by others on each of the different emergencies we identify, and our lack of in-depth expertise on them, we limit this section to brief overviews of each to highlight relevant points, rather than deep dives into the effects of large socioeconomic changes and political campaigns like the decimation of the Rust Belt and the War on Drugs. We do, however, assess trends in these crises over the past few decades and offer our best estimates of their likely trajectories going forward, in order to understand their cumulative impact on our students.

The remaining chapters are devoted to syntheses of how the ISS communities we studied have responded to the pandemic, and how their policies and practices are shaping their efforts going forward. We also supplement this information with data from other ISS communities we have studied in recent years, where relevant. These chapters illustrate the school communities' capacity to compensate for these emergency impacts and to support children, families, teachers, and schools so that students could receive a quality education and have a positive social-emotional experience, even in crisis situations.

This book builds on the related work in *Broader, Bolder, Better: How Schools and Communities Help Students Overcome the Disadvantages of Poverty* (2019) and shines a spotlight on the unique strategies each school community has adopted, based on its specific characteristics: size, geography, demographics, available community partners, and culture, among others. We strongly believe that certain types of decisions are best made at the local level, and we affirm here the benefits of marrying that local control with appropriate state and federal policies and support.

This research also affirms our longstanding belief that because certain emergencies with which the nation is currently contending can no longer be overlooked by our schools and surrounding social support systems, our educational frameworks need to adapt and address them directly in the same manner as the ISS approaches adopted by the communities we've studied. Our hope is that the lessons identified here will spur some early change, including enhanced recognition by key policy makers of the value of ISS schools, with resultant increases for them in federal and state education budgeting and additional support through other government actions. We highlight these communities to suggest practical steps that can be taken in school communities and by education stakeholders, and hope this leads to the proliferation of ISS approaches across the country. After all, the better the ability of our school communities to contend with crises, the better our ability as a nation to do so as well.

# 1

## The Reality of "Education in Emergencies" in the United States

THE CONCEPT OF "EDUCATION IN EMERGENCIES" has largely been seen by Americans—to the extent they are aware of the phenomenon and/or the term—as relating to situations in other countries. These countries in which education is provided in such contexts, and where studies of the framework have been situated, are often ravaged by war, serving as homes to refugees, or have been consumed by drought or floods. Some might argue that these emergencies have not seemed to apply to us. But, in fact, most US regions and communities have experienced many of the same, or analogous, situations. Droughts and floods, for instance, have consumed US communities, too—as far back as the Dust Bowl and as recently as the devastation caused by Hurricanes Harvey and Lee to large swaths of Houston and South Florida, respectively. And, due to ongoing economic instability, growing gun violence, and rapidly accelerating climate change, these emergencies are becoming increasingly common. In other words, while, historically, Americans have largely watched wars in other parts of the world from the comfort of our home screens, in recent decades, "wars" of other kinds have wrought huge destruction on many communities and entire regions of the United States.

Though we could go back much further in US history, this book focuses on emergencies that have crystallized in what we consider our recent past—roughly the past five decades—that is, the period, starting in the 1970s, in which the parents, grandparents, teachers, and school and district leaders of today's students have grown up.

The term "emergency" has slightly varying definitions, depending on the source, but essentially it is an "urgent need for assistance or relief," usually due to "an unforeseen combination of circumstances or the resulting state."[1] While some of the various situations we discuss can be viewed as "unforeseeable," others have been increasing over time either independently or as effects of other crises, such as the roaring mental health epidemic and the increase in school shootings. Despite their consistent rise, however, these emergencies are often treated as "unforeseeable" by policy makers and other decision makers. This framing has served as a rationale for reactive policy-making, at best, or, in many cases, inaction. In our view, there can be little doubt that these emergencies are often predictable and require urgent attention—not just because of their impact on education, although that is certainly a compelling reason.

This chapter describes some of these devastating emergencies, both man-made and those stemming from natural disasters, that, while familiar to most of us on some level, are rarely discussed in the context of challenges facing our schools, educators, and students. Moreover, the notion that America is "exceptional," and thus not subject to the challenges facing other nations, hinders enacting policies that could directly address the many crises we face. As we describe below, emergencies on par with global crises do exist here at home, and US school communities have been struggling to educate while confronting them for longer than many have imagined.

## INTERACTING IMPACTS OF EMERGENCIES

These emergencies, while distinct, also interact with one another in multiple ways and, as such, serve to exacerbate one another. Unstable family economic circumstances are one driver of mental and emotional health challenges, for example, which, in turn, combined with the lack of gun-control measures, contribute to the gun-violence epidemic increasingly plaguing urban, rural, and even suburban communities across the country. Similarly, while climate change is, on the surface, unrelated to the economic stressors described, the accumulated economic instability and mental health crises limit these communities' physical resources and social-emotional capacity to contend with climate-induced natural disasters. The cumulative effects of these multiple stressors inevitably build up, with one compounding others.

With this perspective, it's clear that business-as-usual education, including the types of education reform in which we have engaged in recent decades, is not sufficient to address the enormous problems we face. Nor is this how a nation serious about its educational future would respond to emergencies.

Next, we discuss several of these recent, pressing emergencies and their impacts that, we argue, drive the need for more schools to employ integrated student supports (ISS) in the United States. In assessing research about the types of crises schools must confront, we came to the conclusion that they generally fall into three broad categories:

1. The Emergency of Economic Instability
2. The Emergency of Climate Change
3. The Emergency of Mental Health Challenges

Within each category, we isolate specific aspects that directly and/or indirectly affect schools' ability to educate and students' capacities to learn. While these three categories are distinct in many ways, they also overlap, often inextricably. We thus argue the necessity of employing a similarly multifaceted strategy to address them: ISS.

## 1. THE EMERGENCY OF ECONOMIC INSTABILITY

As substantial literature has documented, and as the sections below illustrate, poverty in the United States has long posed a major impediment to parents' success in raising healthy, happy, thriving children, and to teachers' and schools' success in developing healthy, happy, and well-educated students. Using the relative measure employed by the Organisation for Economic Co-operation and Development (OECD), the rate of US child poverty has been documented as being much higher than those of nations we consider our peers: at over 20 percent in 2021, our percentage stands slightly higher than those of Mexico and Bulgaria (two of the poorest OECD nations), nearly twice the OECD average of around 12 percent, and roughly five times that of the least poor nation, Finland.[2]

Children, and thus schools, in the United States face another challenge—both absolute and relative—to effective teaching and learning: a skimpy, uneven, and tattered social safety net. In contrast to our European and Canadian counterparts, US families have never enjoyed the benefits of a capitalism that is cushioned by strong social insurance and other family-friendly public policies. Our unique lack of any mandated paid leave for the birth or adoption of a child, or paid sick leave to care for said child, and our limited and unaffordable child care or early education severely impact families and teachers alike.

In 1964, when President Lyndon B. Johnson declared an "unconditional war on poverty," the country's poor were already experiencing high levels of economic distress.[3] Evidence shows that the major public assistance programs initiated during that time, such as the Food Stamp Program, later renamed the Supplemental Nutrition Assistance Program (SNAP), and social insurance programs, such as Unemployment Insurance, successfully helped millions of Americans to climb out of poverty. And they have continued to do so, with particularly significant benefit during economic crises such as the Great Recession of 2008.[4] In a 2016 report, the US Department of Health and Human Services found that over the fifty years since their initiation, these programs have been the largest factor contributing to the reduction of the national poverty rate.[5]

Yet, despite programs that have made recessions less severe and kept millions of people out of poverty, over the past fifty years economic inequality has increased between families in the lowest and highest income levels.[6] Women, Black, Indigenous, and other people of color are disproportionately represented among the Americans in need of these programs.[7] The programs are insufficient relative to US levels of need, with resources for many of them cut in recent decades and requirements to access them often in conflict with one another. Moreover, stagnating wages and growing income and wealth inequality mean that many Americans must utilize one or more of these programs concurrently to make ends meet, and millions still live in poverty.[8]

Scholars of poverty and social programs find that these gaps and disparities are due in large part to the inadequate and uneven nature of the United States' current social safety net programs—especially when compared to peer nations. For example, in their comparative study, Rebecca Blank and Maria Hanratty found that Canada's social safety net system, which is much more expansive in its eligibility requirements and offers higher levels of benefits, provides more protection against poverty and, if applied in the US context, would substantially lower poverty rates and gaps.[9]

In fact, many of the socioeconomic challenges the United States has faced since the 1960s—job loss, food insecurity, homelessness, and parental absence, all of which are indicators of economic crisis and instability—have reached emergency levels. The country's lack of adequate and adaptive social safety nets has exacerbated such situations for many, with ripple effects on communities and schools.

## 1.1 Employment

We see this acutely with employment. Secure employment with a living wage is at the core of stability in a capitalist economy. Sudden job loss, especially in high numbers and/or concentrated regions, can shock a community in ways that can be hard, if not impossible, to recover from. Although the United States had become a world leader and economic powerhouse by the mid-1960s, at the height of the Cold War, a seismic shift in the manufacturing industry caused sudden and staggering job loss in certain communities across the country. Mass factory closures began around 1970 and accelerated through the 1980s, creating a downward economic spiral, with effects highly concentrated in many of the cities and communities that had enjoyed the greatest growth and prosperity in prior decades. Communities across the "Steel Belt"—running from Ohio through Pennsylvania and into Wisconsin—and the "Automobile Belt"—concentrated in Michigan, Ohio, and Indiana—devolved from economic bright spots into an increasingly blighted "Rust Belt."

While the total number of US manufacturing jobs actually rose slightly during this period, from 20.1 million in 1973 to 20.3 million in 1980, as a share of the economy, manufacturing declined substantially, from over a quarter of the US labor force in 1973 (26.2 percent) to just over a fifth (22.1 percent) in 1980.[10] In specific industries and places, the losses were staggering. As an in-depth article documenting this moment in time illustrates, these losses spurred sudden and high levels of unemployment in cities that had recently been among the country's most prosperous, along with mass displacement: "Between 1970 and 1980, United States and Middle West steel production dropped 15 percent; Pennsylvania's production dropped 21 percent; Ohio's, 26 percent. . . . Unemployment in the auto industry stands at 22 percent. Since 1950, Detroit's population has fallen 35 percent; Pittsburgh's, 37 percent. Soon, Akron, Ohio, once the world capital of the automobile-tire industry, will no longer make an automobile or truck tire."[11] As manufacturing jobs disappeared en masse, some of the country's biggest cities lost large segments of their population—Buffalo, Cleveland, Detroit, and Pittsburgh each lost over 40 percent of their populations between 1970 and 2006—and smaller cities and towns such as Monessen, Pennsylvania, hollowed out, becoming literal shells of their former selves.[12]

Some proponents viewed the ascendant cities in the "Sun Belt"—across such southwestern states as Arizona, Texas, and California, which saw substantial population and growth—and the descendant Rust Belt as natural, even healthy, consequences of a robust capitalist society, but with respect to the latter, "for those living in these blighted areas, discourses on rise and decline conveyed a sense of powerlessness and inevitability."[13] Indeed, tracing the reverberations of this collapse throughout a community reveals the helplessness and despair wrought by these sudden changes. A study of the closure of the American Motors assembly plant in Kenosha, Wisconsin, for example, found impacts far beyond the mass job loss. Yale University anthropology professor Kathryn Marie Dudley described the loss of the community's social structure—a culture that had rewarded and conferred dignity for labor was supplanted by a postindustrial culture that valued educational attainment over seniority and physical abilities.[14] As thousands of men could no longer find jobs that afforded them dignity and enabled them to support their families, and familiar institutions from churches to bowling alleys that had anchored their communities lost members and influence, rates of alcoholism and drug addiction rose, along with other aspects of family dysfunction. The spikes in poverty and in family and community dysfunction led, as well, to substantial increases in crime rates across many Rust Belt cities.

A related consequence was the "brain drain" from affected communities, which has been documented over the past few decades. The combination of loss of the more educated residents and an economy that increasingly demanded workers with higher levels of educational attainment led Rust Belt cities and towns to turn to standards-oriented education reform as a potential solution. Studies of these attempts by urban and school leaders, however, paint at best a mixed picture with respect to progress or success. A 2008 study of such a strategy in a former mill town devastated by mass job loss describes the conflicts between residents' conceptions of civic capacity and rapidly shifting economic realities. The authors note resulting paradoxes in "city leaders' increasing hope[s] that school reform can spark a renaissance in struggling communities."[15]

While some Rust Belt communities such as Chicago have rebounded in the past few decades, they represent a minority, and the benefits tend to accrue heavily to more educated and wealthier residents.[16] The lack of social cohesion that cities like Youngstown have suffered as crime, unemployment, poverty, and family dysfunction spread and schools fell apart is a key factor preventing such rebounds.[17] And as cities saw their populations plummet—in the case of Detroit from two million to less than one—and more educated and white residents fled to the suburbs, funding for schools fell drastically in conjunction with spikes in the need for special education, counseling, and other supports.

This combination of factors has triggered downward spirals in many Rust Belt communities, as populations decline and those remaining are disproportionately jobless and living with trauma and poverty. Districts lack the resources to address these challenges and to properly fund their schools, and weak education contributes to continued exodus and further declines.

## 1.2 Employment Challenges Linked to Education

While the ongoing deterioration of the Rust Belt has caused particular harm in one region, the emergency situation it has created is closely linked to multiple other societal challenges, including spikes in alcohol and drug abuse, addiction, and mass incarceration, including among parents of school-aged children. And, as noted above, as both technological and cultural shifts happen more and more rapidly, these types of devastation will likely become more common.

While the COVID-19 pandemic deeply affected the economy, the nation achieved an unprecedented rate of recovery, adding about twenty-two million jobs in just over two years.[18] The lasting impacts of such extreme fluctuation remain to be seen, but one thing is clear: a significant share of societal well-being hinges on employment, and the role educational attainment plays in an American's ability to sustain that employment and, thus, a healthy life, is undeniable. According to a report by the Georgetown University Center on Education and the Workforce, the share of workers with a high school education or less who were unemployed in April 2020 (19.2 percent) was more than double that of those with a bachelor's degree or higher (8.2 percent).[19] The number of jobs lost followed a similar trend; the number of job losses among those with a high school education or less was almost three times the number of job losses among those with a bachelor's degree or higher in that same month.

## 1.3   Food Insecurity

Along with the critical need for stable employment comes the importance of secure and reliable access to food. Hunger can lead to multiple health concerns as well as cause students to be physically and mentally distracted, impeding learning.[20] According to annual reports from the US Department of Agriculture, children and adults were food insecure in 6.5 percent of US households with children in 2019.[21] In June 2020, however, during the early months of the pandemic, around 16 percent of households with children reported that their children had not eaten enough over the last week due to a lack of resources.[22] While that average rate was the highest on record, Black and Hispanic children were experiencing food insecurity at even higher and extremely alarming rates, with about three in ten Black households with children and one in four Latino households with children experiencing food insecurity.[23] Race-based disparities in food security, which mirror those of other economic challenges, were well documented before the pandemic and have persisted through recovery efforts.

In response to the severity of food insecurity, federal, state, and even some local government agencies have instituted a range of food access programs. At the federal level, the government provides SNAP; the Special Supplemental Nutrition Program for Women, Infants, and Children; and the National School Lunch Program. Once again, schools serve as central hubs providing for basic human needs and services. The National School Lunch Act, originally signed into law in 1946, provides free and subsidized lunches primarily for children from low-income backgrounds. The program has evolved over time, with fluctuations in funding, student eligibility, and nutritional guidelines to promote access to healthier options. In some communities with high concentrations of poverty, school meal programs have expanded to include breakfast and afterschool meals in addition to lunch, and a growing number provide free lunch to all children, with no parental application required.[24]

During the pandemic, with many school buildings closed, immediate access to food for millions of the nation's low-income children also shut down, making glaringly clear the urgency of food security and the centrality of schools as mechanisms for support. As recovery efforts continue, the emergency of food insecurity, especially for children and the most vulnerable populations, must be thoroughly addressed, including more adaptive and robust contingency plans.

## 1.4 Housing Affordability

The next layer in the snowball of economic instability, along with unemployment and food insecurity, is access to secure and affordable housing. The US Department of Housing and Urban Development (HUD) designates housing as "affordable" if total housing expenses—including rent and utilities—do not exceed 30 percent of the residents' gross income. The wide variety in cost of living across the country, spanning from dense urban areas to sparse rural ones, creates a range in the populations able to achieve this benchmark.

People of color are disproportionately represented among the population who cannot.[25] This racial disparity is due in large part to a history of discriminatory housing policies and predatory mortgage loan practices, many of them spearheaded by the federal government.[26] In *Race for Profit: How Banks and the Real Estate Industry Undermined Black Homeownership* (2019), Keeanga-Yamahtta Taylor outlines how bankers, investors, and real estate agents have repeatedly targeted and exploited African American homeseekers and homeowners.[27] This systematic exclusion of Black families from homeownership has generationally impaired their accumulation of wealth in comparison to their white peers.[28] And, since public schools are largely funded by property taxes, these patterns of racial discrimination in the housing market are mirrored in school quality and, often, educational outcomes.[29]

In response to the need for affordable housing, the US government has implemented programs for rental and homeownership assistance as well as provided land-use and regulatory incentives at the federal, state, and local levels since the 1930s. Notably, under Section 8 of the Housing Act of 1974, the federal government provides direct financial assistance for low-income individuals to obtain housing through the Housing Choice Vouchers (HCV) program. Government agencies also offer tax benefits such as the Low-Income Housing Tax Credit (LIHTC) to developers and investors to incentivize the production and maintenance of affordable housing units. Although the government has approached the challenge of providing affordable housing options from multiple angles, these largely reactive efforts have only scratched the surface of the known need.[30]

Many factors have contributed to the nationwide housing affordability crisis. Researchers point to the failure of income levels to keep pace with housing prices as a significant reason for the disparity.[31] The crisis became acute after the Great Recession of 2008, when the number of Americans living in poverty increased by 27 percent between 2006 and 2010.[32] Many homeowners lost their homes and became renters due to an inability to make their mortgage payments.[33] Further exacerbating this issue are documented patterns of predation on low-income renters, along with the failure of rental housing prices to change to meet demand.[34] Although rental assistance programs such as the HCV and LIHTC had been in place for decades, as Michael Lens points out, they were "not designed as safety net programmes where benefits and/or coverage increase in times of need."[35]

The confluence of a quick increase in the number of people in poverty, a lag in rental rate changes, and a lack of flexibility in housing assistance policy have resulted in a rapid expansion of the housing affordability gap. Indeed, according to the Pew Research Center, almost half of all American renters (46 percent) were spending 30 percent or more of their income on housing in 2020.[36] Some anticipate that this number will continue to increase as rent prices also climb.[37] Emergent research around how the COVID-19 pandemic has influenced the housing market indicates that homeownership rose while mortgage rates were low.[38] However, a limited housing supply and an increase in inflation, combined with efforts to counter inflation, may continue to strain the overall housing affordability crisis.[39]

## 1.5 Homelessness

The lack of affordable housing has contributed directly to an increase in the number of people experiencing homelessness in the United States.[40] According to Maslow's Hierarchy of Needs, shelter is equal to air, water, and food as a primary physiological need that must be met before higher-level needs, such as self-esteem and self-actualization, can be attended to.[41] Despite the critical importance of housing for a person's well-being, however, and notwithstanding some limited efforts around the country to address homelessness, the number of people experiencing homelessness in the United States has been rising since 2016.[42]

To understand the extent of homelessness in the country, HUD implements a yearly nationwide point-in-time count. In January 2020, right before the pandemic, HUD reported that 580,466 people were experiencing homelessness on a single night, which reflected a 2.2 percent increase from 2019.[43] This increase in homelessness indicates an increasing emergency of people experiencing extreme poverty and coinciding psychological trauma, even before the unprecedented socioeconomic and health crisis of the COVID-19 pandemic.[44] And the numbers just keep increasing: the most recent HUD report found *more than 650,000 people were experiencing homelessness* on a single night in January 2023, a 12 percent increase from 2022.[45]

Among many other social services they provide, educators are on the frontlines of identifying youth who are experiencing homelessness. Once identified, students who lack a fixed, regular, and adequate nighttime residence are eligible to receive services under the McKinney-Vento Homeless Assistance Act. Originally implemented in 1987, the federal policy guides school practice concerning students experiencing homelessness.[46] According to the most recent report by the National Center for Homeless Education, in 2019–2020 over one million school-aged children, or 2.5 percent of all public school students, were identified as experiencing homelessness.[47]

Experiencing homelessness severely impedes a student's well-being and educational outcomes.[48] The most common school-related problems include lower academic achievement and poorer attendance, as well as more alarming challenges including disproportionately high rates of disability identification, school dropout, and aggressive behavior.[49] Some researchers question the extent to which these issues can be attributed directly to the experience of homelessness or extreme poverty more broadly.[50] However, in their study of students in the Los Angeles Unified School District, Soledad De Gregorio and colleagues were able to isolate the effects of homelessness and found associations with more missed days of school and lower achievement in mathematics.[51]

Some studies have reviewed the ways schools currently address the needs of students experiencing homelessness.[52] While wide variety exists in the ways school staff implement support mechanisms, across the board, schools overwhelmingly report the need for more resources and clarity as to how best to support these students.[53] For instance, in their phenomenological study of school counselors who address the needs of students experiencing homelessness, Stacey Havlik and fellow researchers found that counselors feel underprepared to adequately support these students' needs and often rely on collaborations with other professionals to do so.[54] Further supporting this claim, Peter Miller's critical review of the research on student homelessness in 2011 revealed that the mechanisms for support for these students are commonly conceptualized in isolation.[55] However, in practice, students experiencing homelessness are usually dependent on multiple supports. Aligned with the theory of ISS, Miller and Alex Wagaman and colleagues recommend that more holistic networks of support are necessary to adequately address the complex needs of students experiencing homelessness.[56]

## 1.6 Parental Absence

The sixth element both contributing to and resulting from economic instability reaching emergency levels over recent decades is parental absence. Here, we focus specifically on parental absence caused by a legacy of punitive and discriminatory policies related to drug use and incarceration (although we recognize the existence of numerous other causes). In the United States, the late 1960s and 1970s were a time of great change and, for some, one of turmoil. The combination of mass loss of manufacturing jobs and the often-violent protests against the Vietnam War, coming at the tail end of the civil rights movement, prompted many to agree with President Richard Nixon's 1968 call for greater law and order. As part of that vision, in 1971 Nixon declared a so-called War on Drugs. Blaming their sale and abuse for much of the disorder, decay, and even violence increasingly infecting once-vibrant cities, Nixon asserted that drug abuse was "public enemy number one."[57]

A decade later, when he was elected president in the midst of a major recession, Ronald Reagan, boosted by the perception that the weakness of his predecessor, Jimmy Carter, was partly to blame for the nation's stagflation woes, embraced a law-and-order agenda to help turn things around. As the loss of blue-collar jobs continued and the middle class shrank, Reagan leaned into Nixon's vision:

> In October of 1982, President Ronald Reagan declared war on drugs. Speaking to the nation in his weekly radio address, Reagan promised a "planned, concerted campaign" against all drugs—"hard, soft or otherwise." Reagan described his campaign in military terms, using words like "battle," "war," and "surrender." ... "We're going to win the war on drugs," he vowed. President Reagan increased anti-drug spending and increased the number of federal drug task forces.[58]

As with many war campaigns, Reagan's approach included a sweeping public relations strategy that "sought to demonize drugs and ostracize drug users."[59] Throughout the 1980s and into the 1990s, Congress and states thus expanded definitions of and punishment for criminal activity. In 1984, the passage of the federal Comprehensive Crime Control and Safe Streets Act did away with parole in the federal system. And the 1986 Anti-Drug Abuse Act, which established mandatory minimum sentences, codified racist discriminatory policies when it made the sentence for use of crack cocaine, which was more common in Black communities, one hundred times as severe as that for powder cocaine, more commonly white people's party drug of choice.

When the Anti-Drug Abuse law was expanded in 1988 to add "an overly broad definition of conspiracy to the mix," throngs of people convicted of low-level and nonviolent drug offenses were suddenly thrust into the federal system.[60] As Michelle Alexander lays out in *The New Jim*

*Crow*, declaring a war on drugs and passing legislation that very dispro-portionately punished Black people and communities provided a ratio-nale to lock up boys and men of color in enormous numbers.[61]

At a time when many well-paying jobs were disappearing from US cit-ies, selling drugs became an appealing option, and as drug dealing became both increasingly lucrative and dangerous, homicide rates spiked in cit-ies across the country. The rate doubled from 4.6 per 100,000 residents in 1960 to 9.7 per 100,000 in 1979, peaking at 10.2 in 1980.[62] After falling back to 7.9 per 100,000 in 1984, it increased again and peaked at 9.3 in 1992, two decades after the War on Drugs was first declared. Translated into numbers killed, nearly 25,000 people across the United States died by homicide in 1991, with Black people, in particular men and boys, very disproportionately both victims and perpetrators of these crimes.

The facts that drug use and abuse were often not the cause, but a con-sequence, of underlying problems; that addiction is a health problem that requires treatment; and that putting people in prison does not actu-ally reduce rates of drug use or recidivism had seemingly no impact on shaping policies. In fact, the federal and state governments continued to ratchet up consequences for not only selling but also merely possessing drugs of various types throughout both Republican- and Democratic-led administrations in the 1980s and 1990s. As a result, "in less than thirty years from Reagan's election through the early 2000s," Alexander writes, the US penal population "exploded from around 300,000 to more than 2 million, with drug convictions accounting for the majority of the increase."[63] And despite roughly equivalent rates of drug use among white and nonwhite Americans, the incarcerated population has been "overflowing with black and brown people convicted of drug crimes. In some states, black men have been admitted to prison on drug charges at rates twenty to fifty times greater than those of white men. And in major cities wracked by the drug war, as many as 80 percent of young African American men now have criminal records and thus are subject to legal-ized discrimination for the rest of their lives."[64]

As Alexander starkly illustrates, like the devastation of the manufacturing sector in the 1980s, the blight of mass incarceration has decimated not only individuals but their families and entire communities. The removal of large numbers of Black boys and young men from their neighborhoods frayed social networks, leaving key institutions—schools, churches, sports leagues—without the men who traditionally helped lead them. It also contributed to the distortion of social norms related to work, marriage, and child rearing.[65] Black children across the country saw drug dealers rise to become some of the wealthiest and most respected (or feared) members of their communities, just as a growing share of those children were being born to and raised by single mothers. Many never married; others lost their boyfriends, fiancés, and husbands to violence or long prison sentences.

When they were eventually released from prison, boys and men saw their life prospects drastically limited. In many states, ex-felons were and, in many states, still are not permitted to vote, stripping them of a basic civic right despite having served their time. As of 2021, twenty-one states did not allow people in prison to vote, another sixteen forbade formerly incarcerated individuals from voting if they remained subject to parole, and the eleven "most extreme" states even forbade voting by formerly incarcerated people no longer on parole.[66] The economic consequences of previous incarceration are similarly myriad and far-reaching. Virtually all employers reject applicants with a criminal record, so, ironically, the very men most in need of decent jobs and for whom the consequences of engaging in criminal activity would be the most severe—that is, a return to prison—lack any such option. This vicious cycle has created entire generations of Black boys and men who are neither "job material" nor "marriage material," with negative economic impacts on men, families, and communities.[67]

Framing drug use as criminal activity and declaring "war" on it also meant that addiction would be viewed by the public and by policy makers as a problem to be solved via deterrence and punishment, rather than addressed through medical or public-health measures. The impacts of this approach have had ongoing consequences through several generations of parents, children, and their communities.

An interesting contrast to this societal attitude is seen in the more recent waves of addiction to methamphetamines and opioids, which have been more concentrated in the rural, heavily white communities where coal and associated jobs have largely disappeared in recent decades. Indeed, Princeton economist Anne Case and Nobel Prize winner Angus Deaton describe the wave of suicides and overdose deaths from opioids in the past decade as "deaths of despair."[68] This portrayal has both reflected and helped shape public discussion of the epidemic and policy responses to it, which have been far less punitive than early War on Drugs measures; even conservative states have boosted support for addiction treatment, and much of the US public is now familiar with Narcan, the emergency drug used to temporarily reverse overdoses and prevent death. Nonetheless, the flood of opioids has ravaged communities, added to already overstuffed jails, and imposed major costs on state budgets. And children in these towns, hamlets, and cities, like their counterparts in urban communities of color, have lost their parents.

By the 2010s, there was growing consensus that the War on Drugs had failed. In 2011, the Leadership Conference for Civil Rights Education Fund, a liberal-leaning racial justice nonprofit, reported that "according to a recent report by the Global Commission on Drug Policy[,] 'Repressive efforts directed at consumers impede public health measures to reduce HIV/AIDS, overdose fatalities, and other harmful consequences of drug use.'"[69] A few years later, the right-leaning libertarian Cato Institute published a policy analysis titled "Four Decades and Counting: The Continued Failure of the War on Drugs."[70]

Nonetheless, the United States continues to incarcerate people in huge numbers. Of the 1.5 million drug arrests made in 2013, the vast majority, over 80 percent, were for possession alone.[71] Indeed, ten times as many people were locked up that year for a drug violation as had been in 1980—half a million versus fifty thousand.[72] Moreover, the epidemic of long-term debt and even jail time for low-level offenses—known collectively as fines and fees—similarly concentrated in African American communities and other communities of color, compounds these harms.[73] The Drug Policy Alliance, a nonprofit that advances drug decriminalization, describes the cumulative impact in devastating terms:

> With less than 5 percent of the world's population but nearly 25 percent of its incarcerated population, the United States imprisons more people than any other nation in the world—largely due to the war on drugs. Misguided drug laws and harsh sentencing requirements have produced profoundly unequal outcomes for people of color. Although rates of drug use and sales are similar across racial and ethnic lines, Black and Latino people are far more likely to be criminalized than white people.[74]

Scholars continue to debate the reasons for the growing disparities between low-income and higher-income children and between children of color and white children with respect to their odds of being born to and raised by a single parent versus married parents. What is not in dispute, however, is that children living in poverty, and in particular children of color living in poverty, are much more likely to have a parent who is in prison.[75]

Researchers also have assessed the multiple stresses and traumas associated with losing parents to prison and being raised without them. In their 2016 paper analyzing multiple studies, Leila Morsy and Richard Rothstein report a range of academic and nonacademic consequences for the one in ten Black children with at least one incarcerated parent.[76] These include physical and mental health problems, such as migraines, asthma, depression, and post-traumatic stress disorder, as well as behavioral problems at school. Not surprisingly, even after taking into account their socioeconomic status, these children are more likely than their peers whose parents are not in prison to develop learning disabilities and attention deficit hyperactivity disorder (ADHD) and, ultimately, to drop out of school.

These clear connections between substance abuse and addiction, the ongoing War on Drugs, and barriers to effective teaching and learning add to the growing list of reasons why ISS are necessary. The millions of children across the country growing up in households affected by these crises have much higher levels of unmet needs when it comes to daily basics, and a lack of the parental guidance and support that is critical for meaningful learning. In many cases, they also carry deep-seated trauma, which calls for a whole-child approach to education that includes trauma-based policies and practices.

## 1.7 Impact of Economic Instability on Schools

The importance of building ISS into our public education system is more critical than ever in communities that have experienced the economic hardships described above. Although the changes that have occurred have not been sudden, they are dramatic, and their ensuing social challenges cannot be ignored by school districts and policy makers when considering how to improve school and student outcomes. The "emergency" conditions described here necessitate recognizing and dealing with them directly.

Factors that contribute to an emergency situation spawning from economic instability often affect students and school communities in multiple ways, all at once. For example, previous studies, affirmed by our own research, suggest that when a child's housing and food access is unstable, anxiety and depression can result, which may manifest in violent behaviors at school. As noted by the US Department of Health and Human Services, "People facing economic instability often need more than one program or service."[77] As such, an interconnected network of supports—often, but not always, employing the school as the home base for these networks—is both the logical and necessary response.

## 2. THE EMERGENCY OF CLIMATE CHANGE

Climate change is a phenomenon that is not often spoken of in relation to the US education system, yet the myriad natural and man-made consequences for schools of this global emergency are rapidly increasing over time. Climate change is the long-term alteration of weather patterns due primarily to the burning of fossil fuels, which increases greenhouse gas emissions and leads to an increase in the earth's surface temperatures.[78] While the impact of climate change on individual weather events and the exact pace of change may be debated, there can be no denying the effect on all aspects of American society, with an increase in both the frequency and severity of extreme weather events such as floods, wildfires, heat waves, droughts, and related natural phenomena.

Throughout the summer of 2023, checking for an unhealthy air quality advisory before venturing outside became the "new normal" for most Americans living in the Midwest and along the East Coast, reaching as far south as Virginia, due to the overwhelming influx of smoke pollution from Canadian wildfires.[79] Some schools were forced to move recess indoors and/or cancel long-awaited year-end field trips.[80] Then the wildfire in Maui, which became the deadliest in the United States in more than one hundred years, brought home the fact that even islands in the middle of the Pacific Ocean are implicated in this emergency.[81] These stark examples are just from one season.

Of all the emergencies discussed in this chapter, climate change may have the most surprising, as well as some of the most direct, impacts on students' educational experiences. As has become increasingly recognized, schools and all of their stakeholders—from students and their families to school employees—are equally affected: "Virtually no matter where they live, today's children will bear witness to human-caused climate catastrophes," Katie Worth reported in the *Washington Post* in 2021. "Today's children will watch as catastrophes, displacements and extinctions tick up with metronomic regularity, transforming their lives."[82]

One of the best-known and perhaps largest-scale examples of extreme weather's impact on education in the United States was Hurricane Katrina in 2005, which broke records in its flooding of New Orleans and residential neighborhoods along the Gulf Coast. Although the impacts traveled far beyond the region, focusing on the results for New Orleans, the hardest-hit major city, provides a sobering perspective with clear similarities to studies of other "education in emergencies" contexts. Early on, children's advocates noted that serial moves and school absences were prevalent. A 2006 study by the Children's Health Fund and the National Center for Disaster Preparedness, conducted by researchers at Columbia University's Mailman School of Public Health, warned that 20 percent of displaced children were either not enrolled in school or not attending regularly, missing an average of ten days per month.[83] The families interviewed for the study had moved an average of 3.5 times in just the six months after the storm, with some moving as many as nine times. Not surprisingly, evacuee children couldn't keep up with their studies. Four and a half years later, Mailman researchers found that more than one-third of Katrina's displaced children were at least one year behind in school for their age.

The fallout from California's multiyear, record-breaking wildfires offers yet another example. Remarkably, between the 2002–2003 school year and in 2019, wildfires, the threat of wildfires, or the fallout from wildfires accounted for 21,442 cumulative days of school missed at 6,542 schools in the most populous US state, affecting more than three million students.[84] And according to a leading expert on the links between children's health and climate change, during the 2018–2019 school year, children in Marin County missed more than three weeks of school due to a combination of wildfire smoke, power outages, and evacuation orders, and more than one million students in California missed school during one week of November 2018 due to wildfires—not only because some schools burned down, but also because of the resulting unhealthy air quality, affecting a much larger student body.[85] Each missed day had tangible consequences for students and their families.

Additionally, families departing from their homes and relocating due to natural disasters put pressure on schools in other parts of the country that could ill-afford to manage the influx of students. The 2022 floods in Eastern Kentucky, in the midst of the pandemic, wreaked havoc on all aspects of life in that state, but the schools were especially hard hit. School leaders, already trying to recover from COVID-19 impacts, have had to figure out how to combine school populations and avoid splitting up school communities as they scramble to find usable space for education amidst the physical devastation of buildings.[86] The quality of education that will be offered becomes a lesser—and more distant—consideration than addressing the immediate, basic needs of students and families living in such precarious situations.

Like the crises described above, these climate-induced catastrophes wreak havoc on the mental health of all of us witnessing and suffering from them. Numerous school buildings around the United States have had to close due to extreme weather conditions, and various types of natural disasters (and the knowledge that they could occur) are affecting students' learning and physical and mental health. In a recent survey conducted by *Education Week,* one in four teachers, principals, and school administrators indicated climate change is affecting their school or district to some extent, and it is possible that they were only accounting for the most direct impacts.[87] Moreover, these findings are affirmed in other research. In an important 2021 study, which surveyed ten thousand teens and young adults aged 16–25 in ten countries including the United States, researchers discovered that "more than 45% of respondents said their feelings about climate change negatively affected their daily life and functioning, and many reported a high number of negative thoughts about climate change (e.g., 75% said that they think the future is frightening and 83% said that they think people have failed to take care of the planet)."[88] Although responses varied across countries, these results highlight the substantial negative effect of climate change on students' mental health and their ability to learn effectively.

Many schools lack air-conditioning, and others do not have the level of air-conditioning needed to counter the effects of extreme heat, especially as it reaches record levels for increasingly long stretches of time. A 2020 study by the Government Accountability Office revealed that about thirty-six thousand schools in the United States needed to update or replace their heating, cooling, and ventilation systems.[89]

These findings mean, too, that the climate-change emergency has now gone beyond creating conditions in which it is difficult for students to learn to eliminating the opportunity altogether, since schools often must close. According to the National Oceanic and Air Administration, August 2023, the start of the 2023–2024 US school year, was the hottest August in its 174 years of temperature record-keeping.[90]

As with every crisis described in this chapter, this problem is especially prevalent in schools serving Black and Brown students, which are less likely to be air-conditioned. As a result of the continued heat wave into September 2023, students at dozens of Philadelphia schools without air-conditioning were dismissed midday due to "extreme heat" conditions.[91] Similarly, in Baltimore, students in schools without air-conditioning were released early or, in some cases, moved to remote learning.[92] Both of these school districts, like many others with substandard air-conditioning systems, have student bodies comprised of a majority of Black students, and this pattern of failure to invest sufficiently in infrastructure upgrades has had lasting consequences. A study reported in the *American Economic Journal* has indicated that the variation in test scores between white and Black and Brown students can at least partially be explained by access or lack thereof to air-conditioning.[93]

The inability to engage in outdoor recreational activities during school hours is another negative outcome of climate change. Due to poor air quality and/or severe heat or cold, students are deprived of the opportunity to engage in developmentally important play and exercise. The school built environment, comprising both building infrastructure and grounds, is critically important and can promote health or introduce harmful exposures that significantly impact children's well-being.[94] Climate change can make existing problems in schools worse (e.g., declining indoor air quality due to mold growth or increased risk of exposure to debris or toxic building materials after flooding), and evidence suggests the potential for climate change to introduce environmental hazards.[95]

Such disasters, made more frequent and extreme by climate change, bring dramatic social and economic impacts for families and communities. Climate change, as manifested in the various ways described above, has created a range of challenges for schools. From an infrastructure standpoint, districts are confronted with the need to build replacement schools for those destroyed or at least repair those that are still serviceable; to retrofit and modernize existing and older functional buildings to address severe heat; or to figure out how to make the best of inadequate facilities. Inevitably, these all disrupt learning experiences for students, with attendant consequences for their educational outcomes. If students cannot physically attend a school, the alternative options include online learning—which, for underserved communities, can be a particular problem due to the "digital divide"—or not attending school at all until the situation improves. When attendance is possible in person, teachers may be confronted with students who are too hot or too cold to be in an optimal learning mode, not to mention the toll on effective instruction. Beyond the physical impacts on schools and students, climate change may also have mental health consequences as these climate-induced disruptions may spur anxiety and other social emotional challenges.

Financially, many schools are having to utilize their budgets for repairs or construction instead of for educational resources, such as additional teachers, IT equipment, or professional development. The lack of available funding for the core mission of a school inevitably exacerbates the emergency caused by the physical effects of climate change.

## 3. THE EMERGENCY OF MENTAL HEALTH CHALLENGES

In recent decades, the mental health of our school-age population has suffered a significant decline, as evidenced by a wealth of statistics collected by the US government and other researchers. The Centers for Disease Control (CDC)'s Youth Risk Behavior Surveillance System established the existence of the trend based on nearly thirty years of data collected from high school and middle school student surveys administered from 1991 to 2019.[96] The report shows that "nearly all indicators of poor mental health and suicidal thoughts and behaviors increased from 2011–2021."[97] Those indicators include self-reported "persistent feelings of sadness or hopelessness," experiences of poor mental health, seriously considering suicide, and making a suicide plan.[98] In fact, according to the American Academy of Pediatrics, "by 2018, suicide was the second leading cause of death for youths ages 10–24 years."[99] The mental health emergency is not only affecting the lives of many American youths, it's ending them.

The COVID-19 pandemic further exacerbated the situation. In a study analyzing data from CDC's Adolescent Behaviors and Experiences Survey conducted between January and June 2021 to determine how students experienced the pandemic, researchers found that "an estimated 36.9% of public-school students nationwide experienced poor mental health during the pandemic, and during the 12 months before the survey, 43.9% experienced persistent feelings of sadness or hopelessness, 19.8% seriously considered attempting suicide, and 9.1% attempted suicide."[100]

In 2021, the undeniable trends preceding and during the pandemic led the American Academy of Pediatrics, the American Academy of Child and Adolescent Psychiatry, and the Children's Hospital Association to jointly declare a national emergency in children's mental health, one that all schools are confronting to one degree or another.[101] Researchers have found that multiple interacting causes for this alarming trend include growing economic stressors on students and their families; direct and indirect exposure to gun violence; engagement in social media with its attendant consequences; direct exposure to climate change impacts; issues related to gender and racial identity; and academic-related pressures, such as the effort to gain admission to select secondary and postsecondary schools.

Collectively, these stressors substantially impede students' ability to successfully navigate school and succeed in their studies. Moreover, during and since the pandemic, students have accrued additional challenges, including isolation, difficult social interactions, and pressure to make up for academic progress lost. In addition to the social and emotional impacts on individual students and their families, these phenomena have also impacted the educators in our schools, raising mental health issues for them as well. A January 2022 RAND Corporation survey found that more than a quarter of teachers reported symptoms of depression, and nearly three-fourths reported experiencing frequent job-related stress.[102] As a result, the social and emotional well-being of both students and staff, along with handling the fallout from their deterioration, has arguably become the top priority of school leaders over the past several years.

## 3.1 The Effects of Economic Pressures on Mental Health

Researchers have established that economic stressors can strain family relationships, potentially leading to increased conflict and dysfunction within a household, which can negatively impact a student's mental health and overall well-being.[103] An extensive body of literature documents the degree to which growing up in poverty, and in communities of disadvantage, drives and exacerbates mental and emotional challenges.[104] Studies have indicated that children living in poverty have more emotional problems than those who are not.[105] Moreover, living in poverty for a sustained period of time is more likely to lead to childhood mental health problems than doing so for a relatively short duration.[106] Unfortunately, for many school-aged American children, poverty has been a reality in their lives since birth.

The emergence of COVID-19 elevated the ongoing emergency of poverty and family financial instability. During the pandemic, one study found that poor mental health among students surveyed by the CDC was significantly higher among those who experienced parent job loss than among those who did not (45.2 percent vs. 33.9 percent), as were persistent feelings of sadness or hopelessness, having seriously contemplated suicide, and attempted suicide.[107] A similar finding was made regarding poor mental health among youth who reported going hungry.[108] Another study conducted during the pandemic of more than six thousand US children aged 10–13 found that "consistent with a prior longitudinal study showing greater increases in trajectories of perceived stress and COVID-19 worry among children experiencing parental unemployment . . . the impact of COVID-19 policies on child mental health was primarily through family financial disruption," not academic disruptions.[109] "Financial disruption" was defined as existing when anyone in the household lost wages, sales, or work, a widespread phenomenon during the pandemic.

## 3.2 The Threat and Experience of Gun Violence

As a core component of their mission to educate, schools aim to provide a safe place for students. However, this sense of safety has been irreparably damaged by the frequency and severity of school shootings since the late 1990s, beginning with the 1999 attack at Columbine High School in Colorado. The school shooting epidemic is a uniquely American experience and emergency; the number of school shootings in this country dwarfs those in every comparably industrialized nation, even when accounting for population size.[110] And that number is consistently rising, with a growing share of US students exposed to shootings and/or reports of them each year.[111] Indeed, mass school shootings have become so commonplace that many no longer make headlines.

It is important to note that while the research on school shootings lacks consensus on many foundational terms, the magnitude of the emergency cannot seriously be debated. Among available data sources, the *Washington*

*Post* maintains a robust public database that documents the number of children who have experienced gun violence at K–12 schools since the Columbine shooting.[112] In order to distinguish among the severity of these incidents, the *Post* excludes any shootings outside of school hours, non-multiple-injury accidental discharges, and suicides. According to these criteria, more than 311,000 American students personally experienced gun violence at school between April 1999 and May 2022.[113] This database is unique in that it accounts for not only the number of school shootings and the number of related deaths, but also the full number of students who, by association, have lived through the experience of a school shooting. Since research shows that school shootings can result in traumatic consequences for both those involved and for society at large, this approach provides important insight into the aggregate of American students who now carry these experiences with them during their daily lives.[114]

As the number of communities impacted by the tragedy of school shootings grows, so do the compounding traumatic consequences of these experiences, which extend beyond students in geographic proximity to virtually all K–12 students who have secondhand experience. James Fox and Emma Fridel reference a change to the mythic three Rs (reading, 'riting, and 'rithmetic) when they describe how deeply the experience of school shootings has become woven into the fabric of K–12 American schools: "In the modern-day climate of fear, the 'three Rs' has also become about risk, readiness, and response with regard to gun violence."[115] From the very first day of school, teachers must now make students aware of the expectations and procedures for active shooter drills.[116] From the National Center for Education Statistics, Lauren Musu and colleagues found that during the 2015–2016 school year, virtually all public schools—95 percent—conducted active shooter drills.[117] While the effectiveness of these drills is still being assessed, research shows that experiencing them has a negative impact on students' emotional health.[118]

Despite their domination of the headlines, however, mass shootings account for a very small share of all US gun deaths. Individual gun deaths—whether from homicides or suicides—are so numerous, under-reported, and poorly researched that most Americans fail to comprehend how often they happen. Significantly, some children live and/or attend school in neighborhoods where violence or the threat of violence is a daily occurrence. For example, in Washington, DC, approximately 9 percent of children up to the age of seventeen—nearly one in ten youth—have witnessed or have directly experienced community violence.[119] Prior to the onset of COVID-19, Black children were exposed to gun violence in their communities at a rate more than four times higher than non-Hispanic white children. This exposure, and likely those disparities, increased during the pandemic.[120]

Research has established that children exposed to such experiences suffer mental health issues that can affect their ability to succeed in school.[121] Whether in communities that have experienced a mass shooting, or in cities and small towns that have lost too many people too casually, children are living in perpetual states of trauma and anxiety, and their schools are operating in "education in emergencies" conditions. Virtually no region and no age cohort has been left unscarred by a fatal shooting event in the past two decades.

### 3.3 The Effects of Climate Change on Mental Health

Natural disasters in particular are severely impacting the sense of basic security of many children. Just surviving climate change "emergencies" has heightened mental health strains. Researchers have identified "climate anxiety" (or "eco-anxiety") as a unique mental health condition that is distinguishable from general anxiety disorder.[122] The former may include "cognitive, emotional, and behavioral responses, for example, to the persistent worries, psychological distress, and or sleep difficulties related to long-term consequences of climate change, and it can result in functional impairment, such as when concerns about climate change interfere with an individual's ability to engage fully in work, school, or relationships."[123]

A September 2021 article in the *Hechinger Report* described climate change as having "sabotaged" the education of US children.[124] An earlier piece in that same periodical, referring to the impacts of the Paradise wildfire in California, reported:

> A year and a half after the deadliest and most destructive fire in California history, students are coping with the psychological consequences of living through a megadisaster that sent them running for their lives. Apathy, anxiety and depression are up, educators here say, along with rates of parental alcoholism, drug abuse and divorce. Some kids still live in travel trailers and tents or make long commutes from towns 30 miles away. It's a collective post-traumatic stress that has turned teachers into counselors and counselors into fire-trauma specialists and left students despondent and disconnected from learning.[125]

Referencing the 2021 River, Camp, and Dixie fires that ravaged the western United States, Caroline Preston noted the threat of fire itself carried with it the peril of unhealthy air conditions. Preston quotes Elizabeth Haase, chair of the American Psychiatric Association Committee on Climate Change and Mental Health, as saying that along with the fires, extreme drought has made education unsustainable.[126] Her words alert every adult who works with children to the extent and depth of the crisis: "With climate change we are always either in or between disasters. . . . If you are not experiencing it yourself you are aware that someone else is experiencing it and you are aware of the chronicity of it."[127]

## 3.4 The Effects of Social Media on Mental Health

As problematic as economic stressors and the epidemic of gun and other physical violence are for the mental (and physical) well-being of students and educators, the significance of still other contributing factors cannot be overlooked. For one, the astronomic increase in cellphone possession and social media use among American youth, which a growing body of research has tied to a number of social ills, including bullying, self-image issues (especially for girls), and the spread of misinformation. In turn, these influences have led to increases in student depression, other mental health issues, and even suicide.

Social media use has skyrocketed in the past decade. As of 2018, the proportion of young people between the ages of thirteen and seventeen in the United States who had access to a smartphone reached 89 percent, and 70 percent of teenagers used social media multiple times per day, more than double the one-third of teens who reported use in 2012.[128] In 2021, Common Sense Media's annual survey revealed that 38 percent of tweens (8–12-year-olds) had used social media, up 7 percent in two years; in fact, it also showed that during COVID-19 (2020–2021), media use (screen time, not just social media) by that age group and older teens had grown more than it had in the four years prior to the pandemic.[129]

While there are also positive aspects to screen time and social media use—downtime, connection to peers experiencing similar issues—researchers have found that smartphone and social media use have led to an overall increase in mental distress, self-injurious behavior, and thoughts of suicide among youth, with especially problematic effects on girls.[130] Social media, in particular, can have negative impacts on youth self-perception and relationships, and cellphone use has been shown to have negative impacts on social-emotional functioning.[131]

The confluence of all we have covered in this chapter has resulted in an entire generation with enormous worries about the future. As both observers of and participants in the negative impacts of climate change, political divisiveness, the pandemic, and other indicia of "trouble," our school-aged youth bring their concerns into the school building and back to their homes, where economic futures may not look nearly as rosy as they did to their parents and grandparents. News about our multiple crises, which comes at students from all angles and all times, only exacerbates an overwhelming feeling of despair.

Other school stakeholders—professional staff and parents/caregivers—suffer from mental health concerns as well. Many of the same factors that impact youth also impact these adults, with the attendant higher stakes of their struggle.

## 3.5 Impact of Mental Health Emergency on Schools

Beginning at the height of the COVID-19 pandemic and continuing to the present day, the biggest and most urgent priority for most school leaders we have consulted is addressing the social and emotional needs of their charges. Two years of enforced isolation and virtual learning exacerbated mental health issues that were already present. The developmental progress of many young people has been hindered, and the result has been, among other things, significant discipline problems, all while the other emergencies we have enumerated have continued.

The mental health emergency is often hitting hardest schools that are almost universally unequipped to meet the challenge. Most teachers and administrators have not received the training, nor should they necessarily have been expected to, that would allow them to work with individual students on the kinds of issues weighing them down. Moreover, tacking extra professional development onto the usual menu of such programs will not turn educators into mental health professionals overnight. Instead, more counselors, school psychologists, and other such professionals are needed to staff our schools, either as employees or contractors. Professional organizations recommend one school psychologist per 500 students, but the national average is one per 1,160 students.[132] Some states are even approaching one per 5,000 students—dangerously short of the recommended ratio. Schools also need more on-site spaces, such as wellness centers, that can facilitate private counseling. Overall, students need access to more extensive services than most districts can easily offer.

Schools are also dealing with the fallout from the mental health challenges that parents/caregivers and their own staff are suffering. Many teachers are leaving the profession due to burnout accelerated by the pandemic, and addressing the needs of the remaining staff poses an ongoing challenge.[133] The RAND Corporation's 2021 State of the US Teacher Survey found that a much higher proportion of teachers reported frequent job-related stress and symptoms of depression than the general adult population.[134] Meanwhile, the mental health issues of parents and caregivers can interfere with their ability to be as supportive of their children as they would like, which is necessary for academic success and families' positive involvement with the school.

Researchers and advocates have recommended a multipronged approach to address the pervasive and growing mental health emergency. Our experience suggests that some school leaders are prioritizing professional development for staff in trauma-informed education policies and practices so they can enable students to continue to engage at school and learn effectively. The ISS model, as we will show, incorporates resources that can be at least part of the solution, ranging from suites for mental health practitioners on school grounds to contracted services with local mental health providers.

The challenges laid out above help explain why too many American schools had come to be in a chronic state of emergency even before the onset of the COVID-19 pandemic. The challenges US public schools face have perhaps never been more encompassing or urgent, while available resources are, too often, insufficient and shrinking. Our research and experience have led us to believe that a particular set of strategies already in place in a growing number of schools across the country offer a robust range of supports to address basic needs; provide academic enrichment; support mental, emotional, and physical health; and facilitate family outreach and engagement—the kind of comprehensive response these multiple crises demand. While ISS are not a comprehensive, sustainable solution to the emergencies we have outlined in this chapter, as we explain further in chapter 2, they are ideally suited to the realities schools currently face while pointing to the longer-term policy changes we need to make to minimize the impacts of these crises going forward.

# 2

## How the ISS Approach
## Contends with Emergencies

AS CHAPTER 1 DETAILED, a series of crises have played out in communities across the United States in the past few decades that have had enormous—and disparate—impacts on our public schools. Although this phenomenon has generally been unacknowledged, underappreciated, or willfully ignored by political leaders, policy makers, and the general public, those on the front lines strive to do what we demand of them. Operating under enormous stress, our administrators, teachers, classroom aides, counselors, and even bus drivers, among others, have persisted, but mostly without the support or resources they need to fulfill their roles. These people work for school districts that largely function as they have for decades, either without recognition that a different approach exists, without the means to adopt one, or without the will to do so. In this chapter, we explain in depth integrated student supports (ISS): their origins and core components, how they work, and why they are much better suited than traditional education approaches to address the massive societal challenges confronting our schools and our students.

In the 1960s, the civil rights movement brought national attention to many systemic inequalities, including those in education.[1] In tandem with President Lyndon Johnson's War on Poverty, a recognition began to emerge that students who came from resource-rich neighborhoods have advantages over their counterparts in resource-constrained areas; and, consequently, that abundance or shortage of resources has a deeply entwined relationship with educational outcomes.[2] At the federal level, the government enacted legislation and made new investments to advance a number of equity-conscious education reform strategies.

Some of the landmark cases and education legislation from this era include *Brown v. Board of Education* in 1954, which declared racial segregation in schools illegal; the Bilingual Education Act in 1968, which established funds for students with limited English proficiency; Title IX in 1972, which prohibited public schools from discriminating based on gender; and the Rehabilitation Act of 1973, which prohibited discrimination based on disability and led the way for later legislation requiring public schools to provide a free, appropriate public education to all students with disabilities.

Perhaps most prominently, the Elementary and Secondary Education Act (ESEA) of 1965 (which has been reauthorized a number of times, most recently as the Every Student Succeeds Act of 2015) offered new grants to districts serving students from primarily low-income backgrounds under its Title I provision, among other important supports. Over the past fifty-seven years, Title I has been the single biggest source of federal monies to address the impacts of poverty on educational experiences and outcomes. However, since its initiation, the federal government has failed to fund this compensatory education program to meet projected need, severely limiting its impact.[3]

One much more recent strategy, the Comprehensive School Reform (CSR) program, which was largely implemented in the 1990s, required grant recipients to apply a holistic strategy to support the multilayered needs of students from educationally disadvantaged backgrounds to improve both academic and nonacademic outcomes.[4] Intended to pro-vide "whole school reform," affecting all operations of a school, CSR recognized that a rigorous curriculum alone was insufficient to drive improved student achievement.[5]

However, the impact of CSR on achievement data has been inconsistent or inadequate.[6] Researchers have argued that the program's failings can be attributed to its lack of attention to critical factors such as poverty-driven out-of-school challenges and the development of noncognitive skills.[7] As the importance of meeting a community's contextual needs became clearer, the education reform landscape began to shift from top-down, accountability-based models such as No Child Left Behind, the 2001 itera-tion of ESEA, to bottom-up, place-based programs such as the 2010 federal Promise Neighborhoods grant program and the Full-Service Community Schools (FSCS) Act of 2011.[8]

Since then, in response to advocates, education scholars, and other education stakeholders calling for the expansion of such programs, the federal government has invested more heavily in them.[9] In one of its few bipartisan legislative initiatives in recent years, Congress doubled the amount of spending on community schools to $150 million in 2023. In addition, $63 million in new five-year FSCS grants was made available in January 2023 to support local educational agencies and other enti-ties working to expand existing community schools.[10] In the early 2020s, states have followed this trend, using discretionary federal monies and state funding to increase their investments in community-school-type approaches.[11] As this forward momentum has built, the need for research to better understand such school–community partnership programs, and the role of ISS within them, is more important than ever. The COVID-19 pandemic's multiple impacts on schools and students, and the resulting increased urgency to address these challenges, add to the need for this work.

One of the hallmarks of the ISS approach is that it necessarily takes different shapes in different communities. While best practices can be shared and adapted to particular locales and contexts, ideally these school community approaches develop organically in response to very particularized conditions on the ground. Thus, the term is used and understood in a variety of ways, depending on the context and other factors. Even calling ISS an "approach" is complicated. Some of the programs that incorporate ISS, such as City Connects or Communities in Schools (CIS), depict themselves as specific models for ISS implementation. Others, such as Community Schools and FSCS, reject the notion of a model, preferring designation as a "strategy."[12] What we find important is that across the many programs, models, and strategies aiming to address barriers to learning both in and out of school through some type of partnership network between school and community organizations, all incorporate ISS in some form.[13] This book explores a variety of school communities that have employed the ISS approach to contend with many long-established crises, as well as newly appearing emergencies.

## DEFINITIONS

Here we provide brief descriptions of some of the key terminology employed in this field and throughout the book:

- **Community Schools and Full-Service Community Schools (FSCS):**
  First conceptualized in the early 1900s to address the many challenges of educating children living in poverty, community schools and FSCS position the school as the central hub for context-specific social services to support the development and well-being of the whole child and surrounding school community.[14] As the community schools movement grew, states and the federal government have increasingly incorporated them into policy and funded specific grant programs that enable recipient schools and districts to plan and implement the approach. In their 2017 Research Review, the *Learning*

*Policy Institute* identified four evidence-based pillars of FSCS: integrated supports, expanded and enriched learning time, active family and community engagement, and collaborative leadership and practices.[15] Other organizations like the National Education Association and the Coalition for Community Schools have similar frameworks that emphasize these pillars and include additional elements. Community schools and FSCS are specific strategies for implementing the ISS approach.

- **Integrated student supports (ISS):** Driven by the understanding that a child's health, social, cognitive, and behavioral development are all interconnected, ISS is a systematic approach that addresses these barriers to student learning in and out of school by integrating into school policy and practice a range of services that compensate for gaps in children's basic daily necessities and "wrapping around them" resources like nutrition support and physical and mental health care.[16]

- **Promise Neighborhoods (PNs):** Chosen and funded by the US Department of Education, PNs are the focus of a place-based grant program in which lead agencies partner with public schools and community organizations to support ISS through the development and implementation of a network of context-specific wraparound services to support students from "cradle to career."[17]

- **Social-emotional learning (SEL):** While defined in many ways and applied in both schools and other contexts, broadly speaking, SEL involves the complex interplay between students' cognitive skills and their ability to manage their emotions and social interactions in a way that benefits both themselves and others.[18]

- **Wraparound supports:** These are the integrated support services provided by community organizations to mitigate barriers to learning, including but not limited to assistance with food access, housing access, employment access, mental and physical health care, educational supplies, and extended and enrichment learning opportunities.[19] This term is often used interchangeably with ISS, though most would argue there is at least a subtle difference.

- **Whole-child education**: This theory of education expands the definition of student achievement beyond traditional academic measures to include a child's physical and emotional health, safety in the learning environment, engagement in the school community, personal support by caring adults, and degree of challenge and development of critical thinking for a global society.[20]

## FOUNDATION OF THE ISS APPROACH

Drawing on Maslow's hierarchy of needs, the ISS approach recognizes that children's basic physical and emotional needs must be met if they are to be able to learn effectively and, ultimately, to thrive.[21] As that rubric illustrates, learning and self-development will necessarily be a secondary priority to the satisfaction of basic human physiological needs. Following from this understanding, schools should not just be places in which instruction happens, but spaces in which the intellectual, emotional, and physical needs and strengths of students are assessed and where a range of resources (school-based and from the broader community) are organized and marshaled to bolster those strengths and ensure that the needs of students, and their families, are met.

In recent years, some scholars have issued critiques of Maslow's work that are important to understand in order to appropriately frame his theory in this context. In general, the criticism has been based on three major, interrelated problems: (1) the unscientific approach Maslow employed; (2) his reliance on a heavily white, male, and high-achieving population (mostly historical figures), whose characteristics and challenges likely did not reflect those of the broader population, on which to base his theory; and (3) the resulting potential for his pyramid to be inapplicable to most other populations.[22] This bias also casts substantial doubt on the theory's applicability to non-Western countries and cultures, which tend to be built on collectivist structures unlike the individualistic societies from which Maslow drew.[23] Finally, as Benjamin Henwood and colleagues note, their findings from studies of adults with serious mental illness who have experienced homelessness indicate that Maslow's pyramid does not necessarily reflect a universal order in which people's needs must be met; for example, people may pursue self-actualization even before their basic and physiological needs are met.[24]

While these critiques offer helpful caveats to guide the use of Maslow's hierarchy in conceptualizing the role of ISS, they do not effectively undermine the fundamental notion that students' physical, emotional, financial, and other problems pose real challenges to their ability to learn effectively and, thus, to schools' operations and ability to successfully deliver instruction.[25]

## CORE COMPONENTS OF THE ISS APPROACH

ISS strategies employ a multifaceted approach, taking into account both the need for enrichment and for better opportunities for historically disadvantaged students. This emphasis on fulfilling both components of the educational experience avoids taking a deficit approach to students, families, and their communities. Rather, ISS scholars and practitioners balance addressing needs with identifying and drawing on assets and bolstering skills and strengths. As City Connects, one of the organizations whose work we highlight in this book, describes in its comprehensive 2018 progress report, "Developmental science points to the *value of addressing children's strengths in addition to their needs,* creating conditions for resilience."[26] This means that effective ISS should specifically incorporate approaches to amplify individual student strengths as well as meet their needs.

The core components of an ISS support structure can thus be viewed as composed of three sets of interrelated goals and actions: (1) ensuring that children's basic needs are met; (2) bolstering enrichment opportunities;

and (3) building a network of relationships that supports both, in recognition of a school's inability to satisfy these requirements alone. Here we briefly describe these components and their subcomponents, acknowledging potential overlap among them. As discussed in more detail below and throughout the following chapters, the specific ways in which ISS districts and schools provide these supports varies substantially.

## 1. MEETING CHILDREN'S BASIC NEEDS THROUGH WRAPAROUND SUPPORTS

Many plans for developing community schools and implementing ISS approaches begin with a discussion of wraparound "basics," and with good reason. The students who are the focus of these strategies often struggle to obtain the foundational support they need to function on a daily basis. Families may not have enough income to feed their children three (or any) nutritious meals a day, so ISS schools consistently provide lunch and, in many cases, breakfast, snacks, and dinner. Students may also lack sufficient or weather-appropriate clothing or footwear, or the means to keep clothes clean, so ISS schools will put in place systems to provide clothing, coats, shoes, and sometimes on-site laundry access. And, of course, school supplies such as pens, pencils, binders, and books can be out of reach for households living on barebones budgets, so schools will supplement what parents, grandparents, or other caregivers are able to supply to ensure all students are ready and able to take notes and complete school assignments.[27]

### 1a. Meeting Basic Needs Through Healthcare Supports

Because they are both more likely than their higher-income peers to get sick and less likely to have access to preventive and consistent health care, low-income students miss many more days of school than their higher-income peers, with chronic absence a major systemic driver of achievement gaps.[28] This disparity in physical health is compounded by a lack of basic health care in many of our public schools. As of 2017, one in four schools had no nurse on staff at all, and another one in three employed only a part-time nurse.[29] These gaps increased during the pandemic and since.[30] The lack of nurses means some students cannot receive the medications they need, and as health conditions become more complex, the risk of improper medication use in school settings—both prescribed and over-the-counter—rises.[31] Compounding these challenges, many low-income parents do not have access to paid time off to take their sick children to the doctor (or even to ensure the regular well-child visits critical to preventing illnesses). When they do seek care, they may travel long distances by bus and/or have to forego needed hours of wages to seek it.

Schools employing ISS strategies view the provision of health care as an integral part of their mission. Some feature on-site health clinics, others arrange for mobile clinics to visit the school, and still others partner with community health-care providers who can support students on school grounds, in nearby facilities, or, especially in more remote regions, via telehealth.[32] These health-care services can prevent illnesses, or detect them early, by making checkups and vaccinations easier to access. They can also minimize absences from school by eliminating the need for students to take time off to go offsite to visit doctors or stay home due to illness. In addition to their benefits for students and schools, these services—which sometimes entire families can access—also provide significant logistical and financial support to the parents and caregivers who need it most.

## 1b. Meeting Basic Needs Through Mental Health and Emotional Supports

Various stressors underlie the mental health emergency in American schools and, regardless of which ones are most affecting students in a particular school, these factors impact students' lives both within the classroom and beyond the school building. Challenged as they already are to meet academic goals, school administrators, teachers, and support staff often are equipped with neither the time nor the resources to address students' mental health needs. This is of particular concern with schools located in communities of disadvantage, where teachers witness the impacts of poverty on their students in the form of both the "internalizing behavior" of children who withdraw into themselves and refuse or are unable to engage with their peers and in "externalizing behaviors," such as yelling and acting out in class or picking fights in the lunchroom and on the playground.[33]

In keeping with their dual approach to build upon strengths and address needs, schools employing ISS strategies prioritize supporting children's emotional well-being along with addressing mental health problems and crises. Some expand their counselor and social-worker staff to bolster what is often a drastically insufficient level of support otherwise provided by their district. Others may hire psychologists to work either in a school-based clinic or out of another office located within the school building, or they may build partnerships with community mental health providers (or regional providers in more rural districts). The services provided by these professionals can range from basic attention to daily emotional needs to crisis intervention, and they complement social and emotional well-being strategies that ISS schools typically bake into their standards, curriculum, and instructional strategies.

## 2. PROVIDING ENRICHMENT OPPORTUNITIES

Opportunities to engage in student-centered, project-based, and hands-on learning are known to improve academic outcomes as well as nonacademic ones, such as attendance and behavior, social-emotional development, and avoidance of involvement in illegal activities.[34] Typical public school programming does not always include such enrichment, however, and when it does, programs may be limited in availability or quality.

Due to inequitable access to resources, families living in low-income communities often struggle to secure such extra learning time for their children and miss out on the enriching learning experiences commonly available to youth living in higher-income communities. The enriching activities that more affluent children experience—such as music lessons, robotics classes, and organized sports—often take place in afterschool, weekend, and summer programs that can be beyond the financial means of less wealthy families, and they tend to involve logistics that can be difficult for more stretched households to manage.[35]

Working with their community partners, ISS schools arrange for supplemental academic instruction, one-on-one mentoring and tutoring, and a variety of learning activities beyond school hours and grounds. These may include free enrollment in art classes at a museum, field trips to visit a nature preserve, or other opportunities mirroring those available to well-off students. By consistently assessing the needs of their student body and gathering input from parents/caregivers, these schools are able to determine which services are most needed and to tailor enrichment options to complement and bolster students' particular skills and interests.

## 3.  BUILDING A NETWORK OF RELATIONSHIPS THROUGH COLLABORATIVE LEADERSHIP

The concept and practice of collaborative leadership is a core pillar of the FSCS strategy and is also found in other schools that employ ISS approaches. While collaborative leadership can take different forms, it often involves school staff, families, students, and external community members playing important roles in decision-making and ensuring that the needs of a community are being addressed. Starting as early as the initial design of a school, the inclusion of all of these stakeholders in the process can establish a strong foundation for mutual trust and joint work that is then enhanced through the creation of policies and procedures that systematize relationships and roles.

In some of the most effective ISS school districts, a key component of collaborative leadership is a designated community school coordinator whose primary tasks include building relationships with families and community partners and, critically, with school building leadership. The principal of a community school, as in other public schools, is necessarily focused on the daily operations within the school building, so the coordinator, working alongside that leader, provides a trusted partner who is more externally focused and serves as a liaison between educators and school staff and external matters.

Collaborative leadership requires strong family outreach and engagement. It is well established that family engagement is of major importance to both student achievement and social development and is thus critical to schools' ability to achieve and sustain long-term success.[36] Students whose families are involved in their school experiences are more likely to have higher grades and test scores, attend school regularly, have better social skills and better behavior, and adapt well to school.[37]

Unfortunately, for a host of reasons, attaining strong family involvement in schools can be particularly challenging in schools that would most benefit from it: those serving low-income, immigrant, and heavily nonwhite communities. Barriers may include parents' own negative experiences as students when they were young; schedule and time constraints due to multiple jobs and obligations and/or irregular work schedules; cultural expectations derived from experiences in other countries; and communication difficulties between educators and parents/caregivers.[38] And despite the best of intentions, school staff weighed down by multiple responsibilities may not be able to focus their energies on overcoming these barriers to family engagement. After working to persuade non-English-speaking parents to attend parent-teacher conferences, for example, administrators must provide translators, and teachers may struggle to hold parents' attention while the younger siblings for whom they could not afford a babysitter distract from the already time-constrained conversation.

Schools that employ ISS approaches make family engagement a fundamental part of their operations. They devise a range of strategies to make parents feel welcome and appreciated, clarifying the pivotal role they play as partners in driving their children's academic success in school and empowering them to take on roles as collaborators in leadership. Often, community school coordinators are at the center of these efforts, but all staff are typically speaking and acting in ways that reinforce the centrality of parental engagement. ISS schools typically take tailored approaches to parent-teacher conferences that optimize parent/caregiver understanding of their children's progress and the ability to ask important questions, providing guidance regarding the curriculum and instruction; translators, on-site babysitting, and other resources; and even dinner to make the evening more appealing and convenient.

Further, family engagement can be enhanced when ISS schools provide certain services that raise the perceived value of school as a supportive institution to parents and caregivers. This occurs, for example, when schools provide badly needed health care and mental health services to children (and their families), or when schools offer annual tax clinics that help parents navigate the complex Internal Revenue Service process and take advantage of benefits, such as the Earned Income Tax Credit, for which they may be eligible. Some schools designate a room or other space for parents to gather for coffee and informal conversations with teachers and administrators and offer classes and other resources that directly relate to the children's education or help parents with their own education, such as English as a second language classes.[39] Whether out of simple appreciation for the school's efforts, understanding the benefits for themselves, or a belief that their involvement will strengthen the school and better ensure its sustainability, the recipients of these services often become more engaged.[40]

## 3a. Building a Network of Relationships Through Community Partnerships

Perhaps the biggest concern voiced by skeptics of ISS approaches, including, but not limited to, community schools, is that schools are not intended or equipped to do all of this work. Indeed, they point out that schools generally struggle to implement even the basics expected of them: getting students to class on a regular basis and enabling them to read and do math at appropriate grade levels. While these are valid concerns, the ISS approach flips the narrative: proponents argue that without these "additional" supports, schools are unlikely to accomplish the basics, let alone more ambitious goals cited in federal, state, and local education policies. Advocates and practitioners of ISS also readily acknowledge that the school personnel alone cannot provide all of those supports, which is why community partnerships are such an integral component of the ISS and community school models.

Partnerships look different from community to community, but they all require schools to find resources that are not otherwise within their means. One area in which ISS schools often excel is in addressing student and family hunger. While the federal school meals program enables schools to provide free or reduced-price lunches to many students who need it, some cannot access this food or are dissuaded from doing so due to stigma. Breakfast programs are far less available and often provided in contexts that their intended recipients cannot take advantage of. Many students cannot get by without snacks, dinners, and/or weekend meals as well. ISS schools work with local supermarkets, big box stores, philanthropies, religious institutions, and other entities to establish systems for food supply and delivery. They have built networks at the community and sometimes regional level to support students' personal and school supply needs, whether through "pantries" students can access in a guidance counselor's office, backpacks that can be filled in an inconspicuous manner, or local store discounts. Physical and mental health providers partner with many, if not most, ISS schools, and religious and community organizations help with tutoring, mentoring, and a range of other services and supports.

Implementing an ISS approach requires a high level of collaboration between the proprietary organization, school-level leadership, district-level leadership, and community nonprofit organizations. Among the many stakeholders involved, the coordinators at ISS schools are central to the effort to identify school community needs, find partners that can help address them, take the lead on structuring each partnership, and then work to sustain partnerships long term. In this capacity, coordinators work closely with school principals and other staff to ensure a partnership can work.

Since the ISS approach seeks to bring together many stakeholders in a collaborative effort, the management of these sites is complex, requiring highly skilled and efficient arbiters. And, as discussed above, such collaboration looks different in each community. In Promise Neighborhoods, for example, the hub is outside the school. To better understand these networks, the Promise Neighborhood Institute, run by PolicyLink, a national research and action organization, worked with Mathematica Policy Research to create site profiles of many active PNs. A figure illustrating the Los Angeles PN's organizational structure, for example, includes thirty positions that are either management positions or groups of implementers.[41] Our research suggests that recruiting and training the ideal people for these roles can be challenging, and that the best people for the job are often those from the communities themselves, with deep knowledge of the local cultures and long-standing organizational ties.

## 3b. Boosting the Network of Relationships Through Leveraging National and Regional Organizations and Universities

Because local resources may not be sufficient to support the operations of an ISS school, a district or school may look to obtain high-level support from regional and/or national organizations with relevant expertise.

The Coalition for Community Schools (CCS), for example, a national association of organizations that supports a FSCS approach to education, provides guidance, training, and other resources for communities utilizing, or seeking to utilize, that kind of strategy.[42] Similarly, Bright Futures USA affiliate districts rely on the organization's national team/office for training, advice, and connections to relevant resources. Regional institutions can provide more targeted support. In New York, Binghamton University has a Community Schools Technical Assistance Center that provides support for schools in the central and western region of that state. There also exists a national network of university-assisted community schools, which benefit from the intellectual and other resources provided by civically engaged higher education institutions; and the newly independent Partners for Rural Impact (formerly Partners for Education) in Berea, Kentucky, works with rural communities across several states to adapt and implement community schools strategies in those unique contexts.

## THE GROWING MOMENTUM OF THE COMMUNITY SCHOOL MOVEMENT

As recently as 2019, those studying ISS approaches questioned whether advocates, scholars, and policy makers in the field were sufficiently aligned to even constitute a legitimate "movement."[43] In the past five years, and in particular throughout the pandemic, that thinking has rapidly and radically changed, with substantial new alignment and growth in the ISS space and the clear emergence of a movement. This movement, which had been slowly and steadily gaining traction in recent decades, has seen a spike in both interest and political and economic support in the years leading up to COVID-19 that seems poised to continue in the post-pandemic era. This momentum suggests increasing recognition that, as various crises affecting US public schools become more widespread, ISS is an important part of the response and will need to play a bigger role in the future.

The Biden administration has, from its inception, emphasized the importance of ISS and, in particular, community schools as a strategy. The Department of Education's statement announcing $63 million in grants illustrates the degree to which it has embraced the strategy: "Meeting the needs of the whole child is essential to help America's students grow academically and improve their well-being. That's why the Biden-Harris Administration is committed to increasing and supporting the adoption of community school models across the country."[44] The Department also released a new White House toolkit to help these and other schools and districts identify and access a range of federal resources to further the strategy:[45]

> Schools have always been the heart of our communities—where students learn to be good citizens, where families come together for a common cause, where towns find pride . . . students perform their best—and are happiest—when their parents and educators work together, when their families get the support they need—as soon as they need it.—First Lady Jill Biden Communities in Schools (CIS) Leadership Town Hall Conference, October 2022[46]

In tandem with this federal support, the grassroots and advocacy movement to advance community schools has ramped up. In 2022, the Institute for Educational Leadership (IEL), which houses CCS, received a $6 million grant in unrestricted funds from Mackenzie Scott, the ex-wife of Jeff Bezos. This huge infusion of resources—the largest private contribution IEL has ever received—not only enables the institute to substantially expand CCS's work, but also signals to other potential philanthropic investors that collaborative, supports-based education is a smart place to put their money. Scott also donated more than twenty times that sum—$133.5 million—to CIS, a nationwide organization that provided ISS services to approximately 3,270 schools across the country in the 2021–2022 school year, including some FSCS schools. That enormous grant provides $20 million for the national CIS office, as well as forty smaller grants of $2.5–$3 million each for affiliates around the country, which will allow these affiliates to substantially expand their work in some of the highest-need US schools.

Because implementing an ISS approach requires a departure from "business as usual," institutional leaders and advocates have worked to develop and disseminate resources to support schools as they make this change. Several heavy hitters in the education research and policy space, including IEL, CCS, the Brookings Institution, the Learning Policy Institute, and the National Center for Community Schools at the Children's Aid Society, have officially joined forces to develop Community Schools Forward, a network that aims to advance both community schools–friendly policies and on-the-ground growth.[47] In January 2023, the network hosted a webinar to release three new resources designed to complement and support this work: *Essentials for Community School Transformation*; *Theory of Action for Community School Transformation*; and *Outcomes and Indicators for Community Schools: A Guide for Implementers and Evaluators*.[48] This last resource clearly aligns ISS goals such as "Students' and families' physical, mental, and emotional needs are met" with measurable outcomes like "decreased chronic absence" and "fewer students with vision, hearing, and dental problems."[49]

While community schools have long been prominent in urban and suburban school districts, rural communities that have among the highest levels of poverty and the highest needs had, until recently, largely been left out of this approach. However, when Partners for Education, a Kentucky-based not-for-profit, received its first federal FSCS grant, it was able to implement this strategy in dozens of schools across the eastern part of the state. Building on what its CEO describes as real success in supporting high-needs students across a large region, and coordination among schools, families, and a range of services and resources that was particularly beneficial during the COVID-19 pandemic, this organization—since split off into an independent entity,

Partners for Rural Impact—has established itself as a nationwide hub for rural community-school strategy and learning. All these developments highlight increasing recognition—by academics, policy makers, and the public at large—of the importance of the ISS approach (and its applications across a much broader range of communities and regions). They also provide hope that the resources and policies long needed to substantially scale up this approach may finally be starting to fall into place.

## THE DISTRICTS WE STUDIED

ISS schools are located in urban, suburban, and rural settings across the United States. Recognizing the wide variation in the environments in which they operate, and in the approaches they take, and that some are more successful than others in achieving their objectives, we made a few key decisions before beginning our research. In an effort to understand the value and effectiveness of ISS schools across the spectrum, we decided to reach out to key stakeholders of schools in different parts of the United States and to schools operating with different models. We also connected with communities and districts about which we had a great deal of prior knowledge, and then some that were less familiar to us.[50]

For example, our study includes two communities with PN grants. One is the first rural PN in the country, in the Appalachian region surrounding Berea, Kentucky, and the second is a nonprofit-led PN in an urban community in Minneapolis, Minnesota. These two PNs are operating in very different demographic and geographic contexts, yet they share some clear similarities in terms of the types of community needs they address. Leaders in both communities saw the potential of the PN model for their students and families and have been implementing it, sometimes in concert with additional ISS strategies and funding support, for more than a decade.

Berea College in Kentucky was among the first cohort to be awarded PN grants in 2010, and the Northside Achievement Zone (NAZ) in Minnesota followed in 2011.[51] Our study illuminates how these two communities have leveraged their PNs and other resources to support communities through multiple highly stressful emergencies, including the pandemic. While we made an intentional effort to speak with a range of stakeholders in each community—educators, school leaders, parents, community leaders, and others—we recognize that there are perspectives we were not able to capture due to capacity constraints. Any missing voices and perspectives limit the conclusions of our work and also offer opportunities for future research.

Below are listed the communities we feature.

## APPALACHIAN KENTUCKY

Partners for Rural Impact (PRI), originally Partners for Education and housed in Berea College but an independent entity starting in January 2022, serves students in forty-three school districts across thirty-one counties in heavily rural Appalachian Kentucky. The first recipient of a rural federal PN grant, which has since been extended and expanded several times to enable support in more districts, PRI also has received eight FSCS grants since 2014, among other support. The entity serves a region that features a heavily white population with some of the lowest levels of formal education in the United States.

## FREDERICK COUNTY, VIRGINIA

A mid-sized district about one hour west of Washington, DC, Frederick County has joined forces with Winchester, the small city it surrounds, to adopt a bi-district ISS approach, making it a large Bright Futures USA affiliate. As the only such multidistrict affiliate of that network, the joint initiative serves roughly eighteen thousand students across an area that includes heavily low-income and racially and ethnically diverse students in the city; whiter, wealthier communities that have evolved into exurban commuter pockets of Washington; and poorer, also heavily white, rural areas along the western areas of the county.

## GRAIN VALLEY, MISSOURI

This formerly rural Ozarks community has grown rapidly in recent years into a mid-sized bedroom community on the outskirts of the Kansas City metro area. A young and heavily white community—residents' average age is below thirty-five and just 12 percent of residents are nonwhite—Grain Valley has a high average household income of around $75,000. Notwithstanding the district's low overall poverty rate, however, the level of need varies substantially across the schools served by the Bright Futures USA ISS program.

## MINNEAPOLIS, MINNESOTA

The low-income, heavily African American section of North Minneapolis has been dubbed "Murderopolis" due to its historically high rate of violent crime. Modeled on the Harlem Children's Zone in New York City, NAZ leverages federal PN grants, along with other streams of funding, to serve a thirteen-neighborhood area comprising sixty-seven thousand residents, 92 percent of whom are people of color living in an otherwise heavily white city. NAZ partners with more than twenty-five schools—public, charter, and private parochial (Catholic)—and with dozens of local/community organizations that support those schools' students and families. For example, Ascension Catholic School has served North Minneapolis since 1897 but, as Principal Benito Matias notes in chapter VII, it has gone through many cycles of change in that time. Of the

FIGURE 2.1 Details about our five ISS communities

current student body, 95 percent live within a five-mile radius, virtually all (90–95 percent) are students of color, a large majority (70–80 percent) qualify for free or reduced-price meals, and half of NAZ students test below grade level in math and/or reading.

## SALEM, MASSACHUSETTS

This small New England city, formerly a fishing town, and best known as the site of the 1692 witch trials, is today a diverse exurb of the Boston metro area and popular tourist destination. The district's schools serve a relatively low-income student body that is increasingly Hispanic and immigrant. Two ISS programs—City Connects and the EdRedesign Lab—work jointly to support students and their families across a range of areas, with the mayor and a Children's Cabinet (see chapter 3) at the center of those efforts.

TABLE 2.1 Demographic details about our five ISS communities

| District | ISS approach(es) | Community type | Number of students | Demographics | | |
|---|---|---|---|---|---|---|
| Berea/ Appalachian Kentucky | Promise Neighborhoods, Community School, Partners for Rural Impact (previously Partners for Education) | Extremely rural; 43 school districts spread over 31 eastern Appalachian counties. | 64,487 | Counties = 31. School districts = 43. Total students represented = 64,487. Demographic breakdowns: | | |
| | | | | *Race* | *Count* | *%* |
| | | | | American Indian or Alaska Native | 50 | 0.08 |
| | | | | Asian | 202 | 0.31 |
| | | | | Black | 774 | 1.20 |
| | | | | Hispanic or Latino | 1534 | 2.38 |
| | | | | Native Hawaiian or other Pacific Islander | 41 | 0.06 |
| | | | | Two or more races | 1,105 | 1.71 |
| | | | | White | 60,781 | 94.25 |
| | | | | *Gender* | *Count* | *%* |
| | | | | Female | 31255 | 48.47 |
| | | | | Male | 33232 | 51.53 |
| | | | | *Economic* | *Count* | *%* |
| | | | | Full-price | 18,657 | 28.93 |
| | | | | Free and reduced-price | 45,830 | 71.07 |

*(continued)*

TABLE 2.1 (continued)

| District | ISS approach(es) | Community type | Number of students | Demographics |
|---|---|---|---|---|
| Frederick County and Winchester, Virginia | Bright Futures USA | Suburban, rural, and small urban | 14,000 + 4,000 = 18,000. | *Frederick:* 68% white, 21% Hispanic, 4% Black. 2016–2021: 13% increase in special ed., 17% increase in English language learners (ELLs). *Winchester:* Race/ethnicity: 41% Hispanic, 38% white, 11% Black. |
| Grain Valley, Missouri | Bright Futures USA | Suburban and rural | 4,517 (doubled in the past decade) | Race/ethnicity: 83% white, 5% Black, 5% Hispanic, 5% multiracial (not of Hispanic origin). 22% ELLs; 26 languages spoken; 77% free and reduced-price meals; 14% special ed.; Individual Education Plans: 13.88%; ELLs: 1.31%. |
| Northside Achievement Zone (NAZ), North Minneapolis | Promise Neighborhoods | Urban/large city | 67,000 residents | 92% people of color:<br>• 78% Black<br>• 9% Hispanic/Latino<br>• 7% not reported<br>• 4% multiracial<br>• 1% American Indian or Alaskan Native<br>• 1% white. |

| Salem, Massachusetts | City Connects, EdRedesign Lab | Urban/small town | 3,700 (2018) | 2022: 68% of NAZ families make less than $30,000 a year:<br>• 27%: $0–9,999<br>• 22%: $10,000–19,999<br>• 19%: $20,000–29,000<br>• 19%: $30,000–49,000<br>• 2%: $50,000–69,000<br>• 1%: $70,000–89,000<br>• 6%: not reported<br>• 5%: prefer not to answer.<br><br>38% Latino/Hispanic; 47% white; 7% Black.<br>2018: 50% low-income; 13% ELLs; 23% students with disabilities. |

# 3

# ISS Schools During the COVID-19
# Emergency: Meeting the Challenge

GIVEN OUR KNOWLEDGE of how integrated student supports (ISS) schools and districts have prepared for, responded to, and mitigated the impacts of many other crises, we were optimistic that those we studied would have an edge during the COVID-19 pandemic. We hypothesized that the strategies and relationships they had established would pay dividends during such an overwhelming emergency, and this proved to be the case in multiple respects. The examples shared from the communities we studied shine a light on the power of the ISS model and its potential to help schools weather such unprecedented crises. In this chapter, we describe how the whole-child philosophy driving the ISS model enabled these school communities to leverage their established processes and partnerships to both quickly respond to the pandemic and proactively address anticipated needs for students, families, and educators. We conclude with a list of important lessons learned that school communities may apply to best prepare for future emergencies.

## ISS SCHOOL COMMUNITIES' OPERATIONAL PRINCIPLES AND PROCESSES PREPARED THEM FOR COVID-19

One of the biggest challenges school communities in the US faced when the pandemic hit was a fundamental lack of preparedness for an emergency of that type and scope. This is not surprising; not only the United States, but also much of the world suddenly faced a highly contagious, difficult-to-detect, potentially lethal illness that was rapidly spreading and mutating. We had not seen anything like this for a century—not since the "Spanish flu" wiped out around fifty million people worldwide between 1918 and 1920—and none of our institutions, government or private, were equipped to handle it.[1]

Schools serving low-income and nonwhite students were particularly hard hit. The pressure in recent decades to focus on standardized tests and a narrow definition of achievement has led to a steady decline in resources for music, the arts, and the development of social and emotional skills, especially in those same schools. These so-called noncognitive skills are arguably as important an outcome of the educational experience as traditional academic learning, and the lack of attention to them, especially to social-emotional learning, turned out to have overwhelmingly negative consequences during the pandemic. These same schools also tended to have experienced the largest-scale reductions in their on-staff counselors and social workers, professionals who play critical roles in supporting students' daily lives. The remaining educators lacked the capacity to fill those gaps, which grew during the pandemic.[2]

In contrast to this paring down of resources and enrichment, the ISS districts that we studied had, by virtue of their choice of strategies, generally been taking a much more balanced and holistic approach to education, grounded in the understanding that academic and social and emotional learning go hand in hand and lead to stronger outcomes across a range of metrics. They based their approach to instruction on the premise that teachers can provide much better instruction when they are complemented by, and collaborate with, other school professionals: counselors, social workers, librarians, and nurses, among others. These school communities also understood, long before the pandemic, that many of their students were living in emergency, or near-emergency situations, and because of this knowledge and through a commitment to act, they had already built the structures and processes to address them. This preparedness manifested in multiple ways once the pandemic struck.

After an initial period in 2020 when virtually all schools were closed to in-person attendance, districts and schools across the country faced questions about whether to reopen their physical doors and, if so, under what conditions. Most districts and schools attempted to follow science-based recommendations, but many faced backlash when enacting emergency protocols and attempting to comply with emergency procedures. While the opposition was especially vehement in certain parts of the country, it was evident in almost every jurisdiction. The varied, ad hoc approaches to this emergency scenario exemplify a weakness in the ways traditional school systems are set up—without adequate structures, processes, and mind-sets for addressing any of the emergencies we enumerated in chapter 1. While the recommended public health measures to manage COVID-19 were followed inconsistently across the country, our ISS school communities managed them relatively well, as they were already attuned to and well prepared for health emergencies as part of their whole-child approach.

## AS A RESULT OF THEIR WHOLE-CHILD PHILOSOPHY, ISS DISTRICTS UNDERSTOOD THE NEEDS OF THEIR SCHOOL COMMUNITIES

While the strategies they enact and resources they employ to implement them vary from one ISS school to another, all ISS school communities share a foundational belief that effective learning is grounded in understanding, and supporting, the "whole child." In practical terms, this means (a) assessing the ecosystem in which each student lives, including both the child's family and the broader community; and (b) acknowledging how the full range of children's lived experiences inform their engagement with educators, classroom learning, and peers.

For schools to effectively address the broad range of their students' needs and those of their students' families, they must first understand what those needs are. They must also have a firm grasp of the full panoply of community resources available, as even the best-resourced and equipped school cannot address those challenges alone. The communities that we studied—and others that employ ISS approaches—have in place multiple mechanisms to survey these needs and assets.

One way school communities approach gathering this information is through conducting "needs assessments" that capture unmet needs at the student, family, and even broader levels. For too long, education reform initiatives have been quick to funnel money into services and programs without providing schools with the appropriate personnel support or sufficient planning time to best tailor those new services to the school's unique needs. As described by the Maryland Out of School Time Network and the Maryland Coalition for Community Schools, "The needs assessment should provide a full picture of the physical, behavioral, and emotional health needs of students, families, and the school community."[3] In order to do this well, a specified team of school and community members must invest significant time and energy to investigate, discuss, and create a comprehensive and accurate needs assessment.

Since the purpose of the needs assessment is to identify the types of wraparound services and other resources most needed by the school community, it is imperative to have not only the right people at the table, but also a robust number of them. This helps to ensure both representation and depth of understanding of the community's needs, as well as recognition of a community's resilience and existing networks of support, which better amplifies its strengths and helps it thrive. For example, a needs assessment may identify certain community organizations or even specific community members who are already providing needed services or have specific skills that may be helpful at a broader scale. These organizations or members may then be asked to be integrated into the school community's network of supports at a more formal level, becoming part of the school's ISS strategy.

These school communities have long been building structures and processes to identify various types of need. In fact, needs assessments of some sort are generally built into the initial adoption and implementation phases, whether the model is Full-Service Community Schools, Bright Futures USA, City Connects, or another. Having these systems in place means school communities had a good handle on pockets of more intense need as the pandemic began. In the Fairbanks North Star Borough School District in North Pole, Alaska, for example (yes, it's a real town, and yes, Santa Claus *does* live there), local Bright Futures leadership had already assessed the gaps in digital access across their community by the time the pandemic hit, and so were able to jump into action to provide Wi-Fi and/or devices as needed, while also assessing how that aspect of need was increasing and how best to deal with it.[4]

Leaders in two other districts—Frederick County and Appalachian Kentucky—similarly describe how their pre-pandemic understanding of where community needs tended to be the most intensive helped them quickly and effectively support students and respond to needs as they rapidly grew. Like all school districts in Virginia, Bright Futures Frederick/Winchester spans an entire county, serving a 425-square-mile region that runs from the outer exurbs of Washington, DC, to rural areas in the western segment, with communities ranging from quite wealthy to fairly low-income. Teachers, social workers, and counselors were familiar with the higher shares of single-parent households and students who qualified for free school meals in the latter regions. They had often prioritized those communities for home visits before the start of the 2019–2020 school year, in order to become familiar with the challenges students might be encountering in getting to school on time and finding a quiet place to do homework, among other hurdles to academic success.[5]

Having visited homes in some of the most remote "hollers" of eastern Appalachian Kentucky for many years, when the pandemic hit, social workers, counselors, and coordinators from Partners for Education (PFE) had a good sense of where families were most stretched to the limit.[6] Indeed, in tiny Clay County, early childhood specialists had implemented a mobile preK bus to reach the most vulnerable young children, whose parents might be skeptical about the value of enrollment or were simply too far from the nearest school site to take advantage of the option.[7] Understanding the critical importance of brain development in these formative early years and nurturing relationships with parents and providers to ensure such training takes place is foundational to the whole-child approach and firmly part of the services this and other ISS districts provide. Having invested in family engagement coordinators such as Jenny Hobson and specialists such as Grace McKenzie as a core part of their ISS strategy, PFE was thus well prepared to work with schools to support parents who already lacked any wiggle room—financially, emotionally, and physically. As Berea Independent School District middle school science teacher Athena Deaton notes, pre-COVID-19, three in four of her students received weekend backpacks and/or some other form of nutritional support from the schools within her network, leading to a relatively easy transition to pandemic food distribution.

There are other great examples of how the region was well ahead of the curve when the pandemic arrived. Several years before, schools in tiny Owsley County had recognized that snow days, which are fairly frequent in that mountainous region of Eastern Kentucky, were total learning dead zones for their students. Few had books at home, many had no games to play, and with iffy Wi-Fi connections, students could not even use their tablets to leverage the district's online resources. So Big Creek Elementary School principal Nadine Couch secured a three-year grant that enabled the school to provide every student with a Kindle and acquire access to a digital library containing thousands of age-appropriate books. Happily surprised at how well students took care of their devices, teachers built in a bit of extra time in the classroom to work with each student to download onto their tablets a few books that they wished to read (or, for the youngest students, books that they wanted their parents or grandparents to read to them). This meant that, when the next storm (or, as concerns our study, an unanticipated pandemic) hit, students were ready to curl up with a good book rather than stare out the window, bored, for the six-hour stretch(es) that otherwise would have been learning time.[8]

In Minneapolis's Northside Achievement Zone (NAZ), since at least 2011 families have benefited from some of the most intensive and far-reaching supports of any ISS community. After a family enrolls in NAZ, one of the first steps is the assignment of a "family achievement coach," who is likely to be a longtime North Minneapolis resident who grew up in the same neighborhoods, and even housing complexes, as their NAZ families. The family achievement coach's objective is to learn in depth about each family's unique needs and assets, with the ultimate goal of ensuring their "scholar's" readiness for college and/or career upon graduation from high school.[9] Coaches work with parents to identify resources, either within NAZ or the broader community, to ensure that basic needs—from food and school supplies to utilities and even housing—are met; help students set their own educational and job goals and effectively work toward them; and connect family members with resources and tools to strengthen parenting practices and family finances and dynamics.[10] The latter include NAZ's range of parenting and empowerment courses, such as College-Bound Babies and College-Bound Scholars.

These investments built strong, trusting relationships between NAZ schools and families over time and enabled schools to hit the ground running with proactive outreach when COVID-19 hit. Family Achievement Coach Tatika Taylor describes how, in the earliest days of the pandemic, she and her twelve to fifteen fellow coaches were able to "make families feel safe in a scary space and place."[11] Our interview with Angelina Courtney, a NAZ parent who referred to her family achievement coach as a "life coach," reveals through repeated mention the critical role various NAZ staff played in helping Angelina and her children move forward through difficult times.[12] Due to their relational, holistic nature, the types and depth of support families described receiving from NAZ reached far beyond typical, surface-level engagement—and the impact was clear.

In stark contrast to most public policy makers and many Americans, the district leaders we spoke with understood all too well that their schools have long been dealing with persistent emergencies. As then-PFE Executive Director Dreama Gentry makes clear, for districts that sought to build and now employ community schools or other ISS strategies effectively, crisis is not a new thing. In her rural Appalachian region, the emergency might be persistent joblessness, the opioid epidemic, or increasingly frequent and severe climate-induced floods in Eastern Kentucky. In her friend and colleague Sondra Samuels's North Minneapolis community, crisis is also consistent, albeit different: among other things, residents suffer repeated police and other shootings of Black and Brown boys and men. Highlighting the similarities between the two contexts, Dreama explains that "for us, and for Sondra, COVID was just 'the next one.' But for middle-class communities, this was the first one, so they weren't ready."[13] In both Appalachian Kentucky and North Minneapolis, emergency conditions are a long-standing reality, and these ISS communities have been building the systems needed to contend with them and to enable children and families to thrive in the face of them.

## THEY HAD IN PLACE A NETWORK OF COMMUNITY PARTNERSHIPS TO ADDRESS BOTH LONG-STANDING AND EMERGENT NEEDS

A common denominator among all of the ISS communities we studied was the existence of a well-established network of community partnerships long before COVID-19 hit. The myriad partnerships each community had in place, which ranged across public, not-for-profit, and private for-profit entities, were intentionally designed to both supplement schools' own resources and to fill gaps that schools were not built to address.

In Frederick County, the Bright Futures coordinator oversaw an operation that would have been the envy of any community. The district's food pantry was the recipient of contributions from both local retailers and producers and big box stores with locations in the community, which also provided school supplies and other basics for the coordinator to distribute as needed.

One of the most critical partnerships, however, and a very unusual one, was between Frederick County's school district and its Sheriff's Office. This collaboration paid enormous dividends during and even before the pandemic hit. As Sergeant Travis Mitchell, a deputy in the Sheriff's Office, reports, an important part of the office's mission was "getting into the schools, out into the community, and trying to build relationships with them."[14] His team did this in ways ranging from having officers act as "lunch buddies"—sitting and conversing with students at their tables on a regular basis (and even pitching in to serve french fries when the kitchen staff was shorthanded)—to raising money for, and operating, annual summer camps for middle school students. Sergeant Mitchell and other officers have even served on the Bright Futures board. This multifaceted involvement from a local law enforcement agency is an example of how ISS communities draw from, transform, and strengthen existing networks to introduce new, integrative partnerships that bolster school communities in meaningful ways.

Through the work of school-based City Connects coordinators, the Salem School District in Massachusetts has built up a similarly formidable set of community partners over the years. These include the Salem YMCA, Salem Food Pantry, Salvation Army, and North Shore Community Health Center. The YMCA, the largest provider of child-care services in the Salem area, is a great example of the kinds of partnerships Salem schools had—in fact, the YMCA actually sought to duplicate the whole-child approach of City Connects in its own work in day care, afterschool programs, and summer camps.

Unique among the communities we studied, Salem also established a Children's Cabinet that existed from 2015 to 2019, and both the YMCA and the school district were integral members. The Children's Cabinet, which was initiated in Salem by Harvard University's EdRedesign Lab, brings together key stakeholders in children's welfare to holistically address the wide array of issues impacting a community's youth. Establishing such cross-cutting bodies like the Children's Cabinet has been a core component of the EdRedesign Lab's efforts in the various communities in which it works. According to Charity Lezama, executive director of the YMCA, the entities that were part of the Salem Children's Cabinet developed trustful and productive relationships with each other; they established effective communication channels, pooled knowledge as to which organizations provided particular services or had specific expertise, and were thus able to move quickly to respond to identified needs. This network of synchronized partnerships, of course, proved immensely valuable when the pandemic arrived.

In eastern Appalachian Berea, the tiny, tight-knit nature of its communities means that everyone belongs to a kind of extended family. And because this "family" includes churches—the backbones of many small communities—local businesses, and Berea College, everyone pitches in when there's an emergency. As such, a region that appears to many outsiders to have few resources proves to be surprisingly resourceful and asset-rich in times of crisis, with PRI, in this case, serving as a critical hub to which all support spokes were well connected.

## LEVERAGING THESE PRINCIPLES AND PARTNERSHIPS ENABLED ISS COMMUNITIES TO BE PROACTIVE IN THEIR PANDEMIC RESPONSES

The ISS schools we studied utilized their whole-child approaches right from the onset of the COVID-19 pandemic and then during the months and years that followed to meet the heightened needs of their students, families, and educators. The three most immediate and widespread needs our school communities experienced and addressed were access to (1) virtual learning from home; (2) food and other necessities; and (3) mental health support for students and families. Because of the ISS approaches already in place in these school communities, many students obtained access to Wi-Fi, lunch, and therapy from home with a speed that mirrored the rapidity of the COVID-19 emergency itself.

### Transition to Virtual Learning Was Relatively Smooth, and Kept Many Kids from "Falling Through the Cracks"

In North Minneapolis, when the pandemic hit, NAZ leadership knew that some families would not have enough devices or sufficiently strong internet connectivity to enable their children to effectively participate in virtual learning. Because their family achievement coaches had conducted detailed assessments of families' household situations, they were able to target families in need early and provide a direct line to coordinators and resources. As it turned out, in many households two children would be learning in online classes while a parent was participating in a work meeting on Zoom.[15] A third child might be receiving mental health support from a school social worker. To facilitate effective learning and work in households where multiple virtual meetings were happening concurrently, some of the organization's first resources went to supplying noise-canceling headphones for families living in smaller apartments.

NAZ not only had a vivid understanding of how different families experienced remote learning, a picture that took many school communities the length of the school year to draw, it also had the capacity to jump into action immediately with a rich partnership network already in place. That combination enabled NAZ to provide next-level resources so that students and caretakers could better attend to their responsibilities at school and at work.

As much larger and better resourced districts were racing to move classes online and establish sustained virtual contact with students as schools shut down en masse in March 2020, the thirty-plus rural counties in Appalachian Kentucky supported by PFE were focused instead on revisiting the digital gaps they knew already affected many of their students; they went to work supplying every student with a laptop to ensure they were ready to learn as quickly as possible. Their foundational experience managing needs helped them expand to meet COVID-19's new realities. Having endured many emergencies, teachers also were primed to prepare and respond quickly. Middle school science teacher Athena Deaton recalls vividly the chaotic yet organized scramble she and her peers experienced the day before schools were shut down in March 2020.[16] She also notes, somewhat humorously, the widespread assumption that the situation would pass within a few weeks and schools would return to normal operations by April: "Two weeks before spring break, we told our kids there is a sickness, so we are going to have two weeks off of NTI [nontraditional instruction] days, which gives us three whole weeks to get rid of everything and come back strong."[17] Deaton's team did not yet have enough computers for every student, and they knew, due to their deep understanding of the community's disparities, that many would also not have internet access at home, so teachers took turns running into the office for ten minutes each day to make packets with two weeks' worth of work to send home with their students.

Further anticipating high levels of need during the shutdown period, teachers organized a system for students who needed in-person assistance to come into the building on a staggered basis, in keeping with public health guidelines. They also assigned each student to a support teacher and provided students with phone numbers to call if they had questions about the work that was sent home, wanted help with homework, or had other needs. These seemingly small but forward-looking resources provided students in this tiny county with an added layer of academic and emotional support that was incredibly rare, especially during the first days of the COVID-19 shutdown. And the detailed organization of services stands in stark contrast to the efforts of many other districts: a year and a half into the pandemic, some schools, including "almost every school district in Florida," could not account for hundreds, thousands, or in the case of Palm Beach, ten thousand, "missing" students.[18]

In Salem, Massachusetts, where schools serve a population that includes a large share of Latino students, City Connects coordinator Mia Riccio recalls teachers' serious concerns about not being able to know what was happening with students who were not engaging in virtual class sessions. "We really made it the mission of our whole school to make contact with the families and students, to make sure they were okay," she comments. "So, whether that was through their school email, phone calls, emails to parents," or by using school social media accounts to connect and solicit a reaction from a student, by the end of that first week after schools closed, Riccio proudly notes, teachers, coordinators, and other staff had personally connected with every single student, "100 percent."[19] And, she adds, this occurred during the same week when Salem educators were learning about their peers in Florida who had lost contact with hundreds of missing students and simply could not reach them.

## Ramped-Up Support for Meals and Other Basic Needs Happened Almost Seamlessly Because of Prior Practices

As newspaper headlines across the country made clear in March and April 2020, one major challenge for many parents experiencing a school shutdown was identifying sources of guidance and support to which they could turn for help. Needs ranged from basic questions such as how to acquire meals for children who had been fed twice a day at school to how parents could support their children's educational needs while not only continuing to run households but also working from home simultaneously, often on limited Wi-Fi and in cramped quarters. The *Washington Post*, for example, ran articles that offered guidance from general "parenting tips" during the pandemic to more specific advice on supporting children's remote learning and dealing with increased mental health challenges.[20]

In ISS communities, in-depth understanding of needs, coupled with a range of resources and established networks to meet them, allowed districts to not only fulfill existing needs but quickly ramp up their response as those needs grew. In Berea schools, where "it was unusual to see a student leaving on a Friday without a bag" to tide the family over until school meals were again available on Monday, the systems already in place could be quickly leveraged. Moreover, because all student lunches had been provided free of charge for several years, programs simply "upped it to feed the whole family during COVID" and to add "proper groceries like eggs and meat."[21]

In Salem, Mia Riccio, who was working at Collins Middle School when the district shut down in March 2020, describes positively the shift from being able to talk to students face to face to relying on an outreach system that polled and tracked family needs on a weekly basis. Given the especially challenging circumstances, Riccio "actually worked with our assistant principal to kind of make that [system] a little bit more robust," resulting in a two-part form that enabled both City Connects and its partners to respond more quickly as needs arose.[22] As the Salem YMCA's executive director Charity Lezama indicated, because of the relationships developed through the Children's Cabinet, it was relatively easy for them to make quick calls to the entities that they knew provided the required support and services.[23]

Riccio credits parents' trust in teachers, coordinators, and the Salem School District for the school being able to reach every single student's family during the first week of shutdown, and for ensuring ongoing communication during those most difficult early months of the pandemic. She also points out that blast emails, which are the main form of communication for many schools, are fairly ineffective and especially problematic for harder-to-reach families. In her experience, "I haven't found that sending out emails typically gets a response. . . . It's just not for our students and our families. It's not really a form of communication. So, sending out a blast message is not gonna do it. It's really about the personal connection."[24]

Riccio explained that she and her team used a spreadsheet to keep track of contacts with students and families. Even interactions through the school's social media were included as forms of contact. City Connects coordinators were thorough in their approach to account for every kid. This may sound excessive, but it's not. School leaders, teachers, and staff are so strapped for time and energy that blast emails and other forms of mass communication often end up being the default for many schoolwide messages. Some counselors and similar staff may have the bandwidth for personal follow-ups, but even those responses are often targeted to students already struggling in one or multiple ways. As Riccio and other ISS coordinators step in to fill this need, they allow schools to build deeper connections with their students and families and ensure they can access ISS services to support their well-being and academic achievement.

Ellen Wingard, Salem School District's executive director of student and family support services, describes how schools mobilized to ensure a smooth transition to a remote learning environment, creating teams around tech, access to food, and other necessities as they shut down on March 12 and 13, 2020: "Spring was really about making sure everybody was accounted for and okay."[25] Moreover, it was not just a matter of delivering cash or resources to families, but also assessing the ability to coordinate responses as needed, which was often just as important. For example, if a family needed their car fixed, a coordinator could identify resources both to pay for the mechanic and organize bringing the car to the mechanic, so parents did not have to miss work and lose needed income. Specifically, because of lines of communication that Wingard and others had established with the Salem Food Pantry, the team was able to develop a grab-and-go meal program operating out of school sites which, as we will describe in chapter 5, metamorphosed into different iterations as the developing situation demanded.

In Frederick, the partnership with the Sheriff's Office proved particularly useful in these early months. At a time when ordinary residents could not move about freely or enter certain facilities, the Sheriff's Office dedicated two deputies to work full time with the school district for several months to organize and distribute aid packages for families in need. Also in this district, recalled middle school teacher Suzanne Miller, "within a day of the news hitting that we wouldn't be returning to school, [Bright Futures coordinators] gather[ed] together and pack[ed] food bags and set up distribution and work[ed] with transportation [providers]."[26] Prior to the pandemic, these team members were a "quiet group of angels working behind the scenes [so] that you didn't always know what they were doing," but they always knew where the needs in the school community were. That pre-pandemic experience enabled a remarkably high-level of performance in response to the emergency of spring 2020.

## Support for Student and Family Mental Health Needs Was Built in Almost from the Start

In Grain Valley, Missouri, teachers immediately understood the importance of homing in on students' social and emotional learning and on nurturing those skills as their pupils lost in-person, one-on-one interactions with teachers, classmates, and others. Middle school teacher Nathan Perry describes this pivot to emphasize that aspect of teaching and learning when schools first shut down in March 2020.[27] One tactic Perry employed was to try to get his students to join Google Meet daily to engage in the lesson he had provided, embedding into his slides a recorded video in which he told a "dad joke." He also recalls that the daily Google Meet time that teachers had jointly set up so students could ask questions ended up being mostly a time when kids could just see each other's faces and say hello to one another. He reflected that the social-emotional aspect of those meetings felt more important than the academic one.

Perry, along with his wife and fellow teacher, Alyssa, grew up in Grain Valley. As such, he knows this fast-growing Missouri bedroom community and schools in a deep way (and he is not alone as a staff member with childhood roots in the community). This long-standing personal connection may be why one of his students, whose parents had been going through a difficult divorce in the lead-up to the pandemic, reached out to the Perrys for emotional support during the shutdown. It may also help explain how, in addition to the couple connecting this student with a counselor, their children decided to write personal letters to the child expressing their support. It was a very "old school" kind of communication, Perry admits, but one that seemed to meet the student's needs in a unique way in this case.[28]

Athena Deaton similarly noticed a social shift as the pandemic progressed, with Berea-area students forming groups and trying to meet up online—a big change in how they had socialized before. "Emotionally, kids were very disoriented, and felt kind of abandoned. Especially the younger ones were very upset because they couldn't see their teachers," Deaton recalls. "Kids get very attached, so eighth graders were more able to deal, but sixth graders were constantly wanting to talk to me."[29] In response to their sense that their students needed to see them in person, the teachers put on a parade to wave to the kids and raise their morale.

In Frederick, when the school district identified by virtual means that students and their families were having mental and emotional health problems, sheriff's deputies had the unique advantage of being able to go to families' homes and meet with them in person to help the district understand the issue and secure the right support for students and others in the household.[30]

Frederick County Public Schools also had another asset in place that proved critical during the pandemic: Paula Johannsen, the parent liaison for Spanish-speaking students and families. The trust Johannsen had built up with the six hundred or so families she worked with paid off in her ability to stay in communication with the families throughout the pandemic and direct them to needed services as she learned of their particular requirements. Her work proved valuable not only with the students but also with their parents: she was able to make referrals as needed to community agencies, immigration services, and local nonprofit organizations such as Literacy Volunteers.[31]

## AS THE PANDEMIC PROGRESSED, ISS DISTRICTS CONTINUED TO MEET A BROAD RANGE OF DEVELOPING NEEDS

Having weathered the shocks of spring 2020 and used that summer to prepare for the 2020–2021 school year, these ISS communities' strong readiness and extensive networks of resources enabled them to sustain and expand support for students, families, teachers, and even the broader communities through the new school year while still contending with the challenges of the pandemic.

## ACADEMIC SUPPORT WAS COMPREHENSIVE, MAKING KIDS LESS LIKELY TO LOSE SUBSTANTIAL GROUND

Anticipating the need for community buy-in and a flexible emergency response strategy, Berea educators formed committees over the summer of 2020 to get input from staff and community members regarding the plan to return to school in the fall. This inclusive process resulted in substantial choice of instructional models, based on the premise that the dozens of districts served by PFE are different from one another and would need to make decisions based on their unique situations, needs, and capacities. Many chose hybrid models of instruction, also allowing students who were learning virtually to opt out of state testing. Indeed, PFE's director of programs Amon Couch notes that more than a few parents chose the virtual option for that reason, and those who brought students back did so gradually, with the option to remain virtual.[32]

A major consideration for these educators were the barriers to successful virtual learning they knew many students faced at home. As Deaton points out, "A huge percentage of our kids don't even live with their parents, [and many are] in very large households," so they would often have a second Zoom classroom running in the background.[33] This prompted some districts to offer virtual asynchronous lessons, so students (and adults) could stagger their online hours. Like other innovations that districts adopted during the pandemic, this one proved so beneficial that it has been sustained (see more on growth during the COVID-19 emergency in chapter 4). In Berea, schools implemented "flex time" each day when students could meet with a mentor group for homework help and addressing other needs, and teachers could check in on grades and look out for behavior changes.

Appalachian Kentucky educators also were able to leverage grants that enabled one-to-one technology at the start of the 2020–2021 school year, so every student had access to a Chromebook. In addition, PFE could draw on a whole team of partners that could deliver the laptops to families as well as a tech service for repairs and support. As Project Director Beth Dotson Brown comments, notwithstanding the substantial disparity in resources even among these counties, PFE had no problem providing these basic essentials to even the smallest counties and most remote areas.[34]

In schools supported by FSCS grants, having site coordinators who were already linked to community agencies made this emergency work smoother. For example, PFE's Gentry points to schools' rapid delivery of homework to students and families in communities that did not have good Wi-Fi access, an opportunity the organization leveraged to also deliver books, art supplies, and even toys to families that needed them. "If they are doing their jobs right," Gentry says of the coordinators, "they will already have a leadership table, including parents and teachers, who can connect the dots and react quickly to any crisis."[35]

In Salem, the ISS district went forward with the plan that had been in place for summer learning, and in September 2020, while most schools were still fully remote, Salem welcomed back one-third of its students in-person, prioritizing children who were experiencing homelessness, who were in foster care, who received special education or English learner supports, or whose families needed their children to be in school because of child-care needs. The school district also relied on its partners in this arena. For example, the YMCA established "learning labs" where students wearing masks could go and work with staff on their academic tasks, which allowed the students' parents, some of whom were "essential workers," to go to their jobs and not worry (or worry less) about supervision.[36] Making this resource especially valuable was the fact that the YMCA's team were able to leverage their existing relationships with City Connects coordinators to build on each child's individual student plan. Tutoring support would later become one of the most widely recommended strategies to combat "learning loss" during the pandemic—another testament to the foresight of ISS communities.[37]

This early transition also enabled Salem to gradually shift to a stable hybrid model that facilitated the full-time, in-person return of all students by April 2021.[38] And rather than using Wednesdays to bring some students back to classrooms while others learned remotely, as many other districts did, the district creatively leveraged other spaces in the building—such as offices, which were now free because staff stayed remote—to space students out, so that children could all learn in-person together. These strategies enabled Salem to be a few weeks ahead of most other Massachusetts schools in this return.

## BASIC NEEDS WERE MOSTLY MET,
## SO STUDENTS AND FAMILIES WERE LESS
## LIKELY TO GO HUNGRY OR UNHOUSED

When a fully stocked food pantry is part of your normal school operations, providing healthy meals to the hundreds, or thousands, of students and their families in sudden need is a lot less of a challenge when those schools close down. In Frederick County public schools, those pantries began as a small-scale operation nearly a decade ago, when former superintendent David Sovine first established the district as a Bright Futures affiliate. In the ten years since, Sovine's central-office staff and Bright Futures coordinators have grown that "pantry" into a huge warehouse and its operation and delivery processes into the kind of well-oiled machines normally associated with corporate systems.[39] Trucks from both local grocery stores and larger supermarket chains—such as Walmart—pull in on a weekly basis with containers of shelf-stable milk, beans, pasta, cereal, and soup.[40] Local churches have developed spreadsheets of volunteers who work all week and year-round to unload and sort the items into weekend backpacks for every student identified as being in need. Even the Sheriff's Office has helped with this effort, as noted above.

When COVID-19 hit, these relationships were so baked in that Riviana, a company with a pasta-production facility in the Frederick area, reached out to Superintendent Sovine to ask how it could help. As a result, the school district received an entire truckload of surplus pasta to redistribute. This was not an isolated example. Sovine notes that, because of the district's robust capacity to source and distribute food and other basics across the large community, a variety of nonprofit organizations in the region reached out to the district and Bright Futures for help when the pandemic hit.[41]

In Berea, the state's Family Resource and Youth Services Centers (FRYSCs)—or, as many affectionately nickname the 850-plus sites, "Friskies"—became an even more valuable resource.[42] These centers provided clothes, shoes, and winter coats for many children, especially those in foster care or living under the same roof as their cousins and grandparents (or even great-grandparents). The FRYSCs expanded during the pandemic to provide hygiene products, which can be prohibitively expensive for low-income households. They were "very equipped just to make our operation bigger," says Athena Deaton, who reports that schools operated FRYSCs out of their buildings during the pandemic. One organization provided services to families in the school gym, another in the cafeteria.[43]

In other districts, much of the focus was on housing. In North Minneapolis, NAZ CEO Sondra Samuels shared how her team's efforts to house families became multidimensional during the pandemic when even nonprofit housing partners came to NAZ for support:

The moratorium was going to end, and people were going to be way behind in terms of their rent. This was going to have a devastating impact on our families and our partner nonprofit housing organizations that were providing housing on the Northside. We all agreed that in order for our families to be okay—to be stable, and for our housing partners to stay solvent, we really needed to provide more rental assistance. And so we channeled close to a quarter million dollars to rental assistance. We knew and trusted our housing partners to execute it, because we don't do housing—they do. The process was that our coaches would tell our housing partners which families needed support and they would take it from there.... They knew what was happening on the Northside, and we trusted them to execute a rent stability program on our behalf for NAZ families to stabilize them.[44]

This example shows how COVID-19 assistance programs, such as the rent moratorium, affected both people and organizations in different ways at different stages of implementation. As Samuels notes, rental assistance is not NAZ's area of expertise, but due to their wide network they were able to "channel [their] resources" so that their housing partners had the support they needed to help stabilize NAZ families in need. Once housed, some families still reported feeling unsafe, sometimes fearing for their children's lives, because they had been placed in high-crime areas. Responding to these very real concerns, Samuels explains that "we actually helped people move a couple of times."[45] She said that sometimes the housing partners were offering NAZ families the best they had, but she, the family achievement coaches, and other NAZ leadership were unwilling to stop searching until their people were settled in homes where they felt safe.

As Charity Lezama of the Salem YMCA points out, Salem is a community in which homelessness has been an ongoing emergency since well before the pandemic.[46] Being part of the Children's Cabinet enabled the Salem School District to communicate effectively with partner organizations that could play a role in addressing issues that arose for students and their families during the pandemic. Even as homelessness continues post-pandemic, through the partnerships that have been formed, school coordinators are well positioned to quickly connect affected families with the appropriate governmental and nonprofit entities.

## BECAUSE MENTAL HEALTH NEEDS WERE SUPPORTED, KIDS WERE MORE ABLE TO ENGAGE IN CLASS AND PARENTS WERE ABLE TO SUPPORT KIDS *AND* GO TO WORK

In eastern Appalachian Kentucky, where the needs of families and communities had long been extensive, a year into the pandemic, PFE Executive Director Dreama Gentry had a clear vision of how those needs had grown and the impact, in 2021, on residents' mental and emotional well-being:

> [Unmet needs were] persistent at this point. We had already experienced the economic collapse of the coal industry, which resulted in persistent poverty, with a lot of families struggling day-to-day. When that happened ten years ago, we lost the remaining jobs, and even more people fell into poverty. Add to that the substance-abuse epidemic, where not a single family wasn't affected, and COVID-19 on top of that, and there has been a sense of desperation and isolation. So, while some of that may be lessening a bit now that we are a year in, [the] Delta [variant] is now at peak in rural areas, with deaths still rising, and we won't know a family that hasn't lost someone.[47]

Grain Valley's decision, prior to the pandemic, to adopt a trauma-informed framework lent itself to the social-emotional focus, middle school teacher Nathan Perry says.[48] It provided a natural channel for teachers, with support from counselors, to be on the lookout for signs of students in trouble: "There were deeper things at hand for our students because of the things that they had endured, because their parents may have lost their job, or they may have lost a loved one to the pandemic. So there's a lot of underlying issues that we couldn't see."[49] Teachers were advised to reach out to students who normally engaged but now seemed checked out and, if that did not work, to alert counselors to act.

Similarly, Jenny Hobson's PFE family outreach coordinators were able to shift the in-person services they already provided in Berea to all-virtual, asynchronous supports; and while her team's work had always involved linking families to community resources, their workload increased with virtual learning requiring more frequent check-ins with families under added stress. In planning meetings, Hobson describes coordinators intentionally focusing more on mental health issues when designing sessions for families. With people living on top of each other nonstop, often in very small, confined spaces, defusing meltdowns became a high priority.[50]

The region's districts doubled the size of their counseling services, including both counselors and school psychologists. They also switched to an online program, Summit Learning, for a couple of years, to ensure that everything students needed was in one place. In addition, they added a mentoring program, with every student assigned to a willing adult (teacher or other). Each adult mentored a dozen children, engaging in at least weekly discussions, giving every student a safe, nonfamily adult to talk to about schoolwork, as well as family, sibling, and other personal matters. "That was a really big deal to the kids," Athena Deaton says.[51]

Salem School District's Ellen Wingard points to the creation of the "Hub Connects" program in fall 2020, when most students were still learning remotely, as an important step. Once a week, all children were invited to participate in outside "playtime" for social time and "facilitated play" with their teachers and peers. Wingard curated a library of activities that teachers could draw from. It was complicated to implement, but kids "really loved it," and, despite the New England weather, teachers were able to keep it going until Thanksgiving break.[52]

City Connects coordinator Mia Riccio was in the unique position of having begun with a cohort of Salem sixth-grade middle schoolers who evolved into high-school-going eighth graders by the end of the pandemic. As a result, she observed the usual growing pains of middle school exacerbated, in real time, by the social isolation students experienced. She watched as many experimented with vaping, for example, but because the preteens had an established relationship with her, Riccio was able to interact with her students honestly, learn about their anxiety and need for help, and provide targeted support: "What I have found through my conversations with students is that it's not enough. It's not helping them not vape if they're already engaging in it. So, I made it my mission last year, as much as I could, to help that class that was about to go to high school. [I wanted to] learn about it, get educated, get them connected to programs that would help them with cessation."[53] Understanding that punishing students would not stem the alarming uptick in vaping, City Connects partnered with a program called "I Decide" to give students the option, with their parents' permission, to enroll in an education-based intervention rather than be suspended from school.

In addition, through its partnership with Cartwheel, a mental health organization, City Connects offered students from elementary through high school access to telehealth visits as well as care coordination and psychiatric support for those needing medicine. The latter enabled Riccio's team to reduce the backlog of students who were waiting for mental health services by more than fifty and ensure that within two weeks of making the referral a student in need would be talking to a therapist.

## TEACHERS FELT BETTER RECOGNIZED AND SUPPORTED, AND THEREFORE WERE RELATIVELY LESS BURNED OUT

Another long-simmering reality laid bare by the pandemic was stress among education professionals, especially those tackling frontline issues related to poverty and family dysfunction. Teachers, principals, nurses, and librarians were not only up close on a daily basis with students' personal challenges and the (sometimes disruptive) coping mechanisms they adopted to deal with them, but they also increasingly found themselves blamed, even shamed, in public discourse when they were unable to solve those problems and get the kids to achieve at expected levels.

Education professionals we spoke with talked about the increased trauma they and their colleagues faced during the pandemic, an experience they shared with their counterparts across the country, but also the structures, processes, and resources they had available to deal with it in their ISS schools. This contrasts with the realities of many peer communities. In Appalachian Kentucky, for example, Grace McKenzie, who was then PFE's associate director of family partnerships, heard about secondary trauma in meetings with family engagement staff.[54] Coordinators discussed having to navigate supporting their own families, often with few resources, while also supporting the many dire and growing needs of their school communities. One school system McKenzie worked with had lost two staff members to COVID-19 by October 15, 2021: a twenty-nine-year-old teacher who had multiple sclerosis and a cafeteria staffer, in the span of just two months.[55] Not only were parents helping students cope with these losses; staff also had to support one another. While still difficult, these regular convenings to process losses and other trauma with peers in a safe space put Berea education professionals in a relatively better position to cope.

In Grain Valley, when the school district settled on a hybrid model in summer 2020 for the coming school year, middle school history teacher Nathan Perry describes leveraging digital coaches to support teachers who had struggled with digital learning in the final months of the prior academic year.[56] District leadership also pushed back the start of school for a week, so that teachers could dedicate time to planning, along with an additional week devoted to boosting digital learning skills.

Suzanne Miller, a veteran teacher at Frederick Middle School, acknowledges the difficulties faced by her and her colleagues during the height of the pandemic, but also highlights some of the benefits of being in a well-run ISS school. She singled out the collaboration among the professional staff, the trust that had been built in the building by school leaders, and an overall supportive culture in which the attitude is "We're going to take care of you if something's not right; it's a pretty nice place to be."[57]

In Salem, Charity Lezama made a point of saying that staff at the YMCA who worked with the schools had in their cell phones the numbers of City Connects coordinators in the schools with which they worked. This meant that school staff who needed help could pick up the phone and talk to a familiar person at the YMCA (and vice versa) who could muster appropriate resources and make them feel better supported and less alone.[58]

School and ISS staff could not compare their districts' approaches and capacities to those of their peer communities, but Salem's Ellen Wingard succinctly expresses the innate added challenges facing districts that lacked wraparound supports: "I don't know how schools functioned without that [ISS] base, honestly. . . . [These relationships] were invaluable."[59] As she suggests, principals in schools that lacked established partnerships with key community agencies along with a system to track children's and families' needs suffered greatly, as they had to start building those relationships and networks at a time when every aspect of running schools was at its most chaotic and challenging.

## LESSONS LEARNED

ISS community experiences during and in the aftermath of the COVID-19 emergency, as well as in the years leading up to the pandemic, offer several lessons, and suggest corresponding actions that school and district leaders can start to implement now.

### 1. Have the Hard Conversations

As our friend and colleague C. J. Huff reminds us, the education community tends to be wary of "opening Pandora's box" by starting difficult, but necessary, discussions about community poverty, students' unmet needs, and family dysfunction, among other topics.[60] Until we engage in these conversations, however, schools will continue to try, unsuccessfully, to tackle those problems without support, and communities will remain disconnected from the schools that are central to their well-being, even blaming schools and educators when problems fail to resolve.

When he took on the role of superintendent in Joplin, Missouri, in 2009, Huff knew both that he needed to initiate those conversations and that they would be uncomfortable. Nearly fifteen years later, Bright Futures USA, which emerged from those conversations, helps ensure needs are met for tens of thousands of students in dozens of affiliated communities across eight states. Teachers in those schools are able to effectively do their jobs; community-level poverty is an open conversation with schools in the fight to tackle it; and those schools are much better equipped to help families deal with barriers that stand in the way of their functionality.

The Bright Futures USA story, and the diversity of the districts featured here, also points to the importance of tailoring these conversations to the community. In more conservative regions such as "the Buckle of the Bible Belt," as Huff terms his hometown of Joplin, the emphasis may be on each community member's capacity to contribute his or her unique "time, talent, or treasure." In North Minneapolis, the conversation may revolve more around communal contributions from a tight-knit African American community that has long weathered hardship as an extended family.

Whatever the language and framing might be, these conversations can and should be had. They can take place at school board meetings, PTA meetings, and broader community forums or town halls. As the districts highlighted in this chapter illustrate, these conversations were foundational to enabling the structures, policies, and practices that proved crucial to their schools and students emerging from the pandemic in relatively better shape, with their basic and social-emotional needs attended to.

## 2. Take a Whole-Child Approach

For far too long, education standards, curricula, and instructional policies and practices have focused narrowly on "teaching the basics" and raising test scores. While the latest iteration of the flagship federal education policy, the Every Student Succeeds Act, makes some progress toward a whole-child approach relative to its predecessor, No Child Left Behind, the imbalance remains. Teachers continue to report overwhelming pressure for students to perform well on tests, and educators and parents alike bemoan a lack of resources for music, arts, and instruction in so-called nonacademic or soft skills, which are critical to both school and life success.

Stagnating and, in some cases, falling National Assessment of Educational Progress scores over the past decade should serve as a warning that the last few decades of reforms have not accomplished their goals and may, in fact, be exacerbating the problem. Yet conversations about education reform continue to home in on the relative merits of traditional public versus charter schools (and vouchers for private schools), with the underlying notion that the latter can better instill the basics and raise test scores. These discussions fail to hit on the realities of students who do not speak English, who are living in poverty, whose homes are in disarray, and who reside in unsafe and hyper-segregated neighborhoods, and thus miss the mark on the changes needed to address them (which a switch in school leadership or environment cannot generally do).

The schools featured in this chapter have long understood that children's brains, and students' ability to focus in class, are intertwined with the rest of those students' bodies and closely tied to their physical and mental health. Their educators develop curricula that nurture students' emotional well-being, keep snacks in the classroom closet, and work with families to ensure life at home is conducive to homework, a good night's sleep, and on-time arrival and readiness for school each morning. This whole-child approach makes instruction more engaging for teachers and students alike, as Frederick County's hands-on curriculum demonstrates, and it can even improve the physical structure of school buildings. See, for example, one of Joplin's gorgeous elementary schools, with spaces for fidgety students to refocus without disrupting their classmates and a glass-walled "outdoor classroom" at its center; or the Frederick County Middle School, where students are encouraged to lead group discussions in the library at lunch and have developed their own system for collecting and testing water samples on campus. Such student-centered approaches, which are at the cutting-edge of education reform, highlight yet another benefit of ISS strategies in action.

### 3. Address Mental Health Concerns Proactively

Mental health is a time-sensitive need that quickly worsens when not addressed adequately. During the pandemic, students experienced heightened levels of anxiety, depression, stress, and trauma. The speed and quality with which the communities we studied were able to tend to these needs stood in stark contrast to school districts that were not equipped with similar ISS supports. In fact, the National Center for Education Statistics found that, during the 2021–2022 school year, "88% of public schools reported that they did not strongly agree they could effectively provide mental health services to all students in need."[61]

Constrained by a limited—often grossly inadequate—number of qualified staff, a lack of access to licensed mental health professionals, and insufficient funds, most public schools in the country are not able to meet the increasing mental health needs of the nation's school-aged children. According to the American School Counselor Association, one counselor's caseload should not exceed 250 students; however, during the 2021–2022 school year only two states achieved that goal.[62] While families with the financial capacity and relevant health insurance may be able to seek services on their own, this class-based disparity contributes to the growing opportunity gap for students to access quality education.

This trend does not have to persist, however. Our ISS school community examples from five very different communities across the country—Appalachian Kentucky; Frederick County, Virginia; Grain Valley, Missouri; North Minneapolis, Minnesota; and Salem, Massachusetts—indicate that, when a whole-child approach is implemented with mental health at the forefront, quick and trusted access to quality mental health care can be achieved, even, and especially, for students and families in low-income circumstances.

## 4. Be and Stay Prepared So You Don't Have to Get Prepared Too Late

With the emergence of the COVID-19 pandemic, the vast majority of districts across the United States learned the hard way that the middle of a crisis is a bad time to prepare for one. Spring 2020 showed most schools were severely unprepared, from the very basics—getting meals to children who go hungry when the school cafeteria closes, figuring out how to deliver devices and then connect those devices to Google Classroom—to more complex challenges, such as sustaining (and expanding) mental and emotional health supports virtually. This was reflected in alarmist newspaper reporting on lines hundreds of cars long waiting to pick up groceries in school parking lots; teachers who did not know how to use the new, digital platforms now integral to their classrooms, which also lacked proper tech support; and the thousands of "lost students" whose whereabouts could not be ascertained.[63]

In contrast, the school districts described here have been treating every year like a crisis because there is always at least one emergency that needs to be addressed. They know that when school closes—which can happen due to floods, snowstorms, shootings, and various other urgencies—students still need to eat, so they have in place systems to ensure that they do. They understand various staff may need to take on new roles depending on student, family, and community needs, and that understanding becomes part of practice and policy. And they know all too well that schools, on their own, cannot provide all required supports, so they have spent years (and in some cases, decades) building a cohesive network of community partnerships that can be ramped up when needed. And, as the COVID-19 pandemic demonstrated, those partners view school districts as hubs to organize emergency work when crisis strikes.

Growing traction for full-service community schools and other ISS strategies makes this an ideal time for other districts to begin enacting their own preparedness infrastructures. And given that other emergencies deeply affecting schools—such as gun violence, drug and alcohol addiction, economic turbulence, and the range of weather-related crises attributable to climate change—are likely to become even more widespread and acute in the coming decades, there is little time to lose.

# 4

## In ISS Communities, Everyone Benefits

**WHILE STUDENTS STAND** at the center of integrated student supports (ISS) approaches and the broader effort to improve schools and the education system, children do not live—or learn—in a vacuum. Schools employing ISS strategies recognize this fact and consequently treat the well-being of the adults surrounding children, both at home and at school, as a key factor in their academic success. The wraparound supports and whole-child strategies described in previous chapters not only help students, but also benefit parents, other caregivers, entire families, teachers, non-teacher school staff, and even other adults within ISS communities. This chapter briefly describes how strategies implemented by the school systems we studied benefited many sectors of their communities, both directly and indirectly.

## COLLABORATIVE LEADERSHIP PLAYED AN IMPORTANT PART IN RESPONDING TO THE PANDEMIC EMERGENCY

Despite some experimentation with shared and distributed models, the landscape of K–12 school leadership in the United States remains heavily hierarchical.[1] While department- or grade-level teams might exercise some influence in day-to-day operations and curriculum design, most schoolwide decisions are made and delivered in a top-down manner. Often, the principal sets the agenda and gives marching orders to their administrative team, which then communicates aspects of these decisions to other school personnel. While some districts have started to implement a more collaborative leadership model that emergent research shows might better support historically underserved student groups, this structure is not widespread.[2]

In contrast, collaboration at the leadership level has been crucial to operational ethos and effectiveness in our ISS communities. From superintendents to community coordinators to teachers to parents, the individuals with whom we spoke continually highlighted how important multiple stakeholder voices were in their collaborative decision-making processes before, during, and after the pandemic. While collaborative leadership can be challenging and time-consuming, the resulting buy-in from, and deeper engagement by, community members typically make the efforts well worthwhile. As this chapter and the next lay out, such an approach not only reduces many organizational barriers to effective operations; it can help enable enhancement and expansion of support systems, even in the midst of crises.

The critical importance of good leadership in the context of public education is well documented. At the same time, researchers have also explored extensively the particular challenges of securing and retaining effective leaders in so-called hard-to-teach schools—schools serving students and communities that are heavily low-income and/or majority nonwhite.[3]

As such, the theory of change around ISS and community schools intentionally leans in on the importance of leadership, in particular collaborative leadership. In its overview of work on community schools, the Learning Policy Institute, which spearheaded much of the recent scholarly research in this space, emphasizes this point:

> Research on community schools and the science of learning and development identifies key characteristics of high-quality community schools: (1) integrated systems of support, (2) powerful student and family engagement, (3) *collaborative leadership with shared power and voice*, (4) expanded and enriched learning opportunities, (5) rigorous, community-connected classroom instruction, and (6) a culture of belonging, safety, and care.[4]

The benefits of collaborative leadership, especially in a time of crisis, were on vivid display among the communities we studied. Unlike the typical top-down leadership style common in US public schools, the districts featured in this book reflect a shared leadership approach in which teachers have a central seat at the table, school staff weigh in as teams on critical issues, and parents and community leaders often also take on key roles, depending on the issue at hand.

In Appalachian Kentucky, where middle school science teacher Athena Deaton describes the tight-knit community where she works as akin to a large extended family, school staff took the initiative to reassign themselves new roles as schools shut down in March 2020 due to the pandemic and their normal tasks—driving buses, cooking, janitorial— no longer pertained. Rather than being told by school or district leaders what responsibilities they should take on, Deaton and her colleagues worked as a collaborative team to both staff up food deliveries to families and create a parking-lot assembly line to stuff trunks with bags of groceries.[5] This enabled the entire school to pivot quickly so that every child—as well as family members—would continue to receive the food the school would otherwise have provided, and more.

The effort described above triggered a cascade of actions, with community members independently identifying and filling gaps in services that Partners for Education (PFE, known as Partners for Rural Impact since 2022) was working to provide. While PFE was able to develop a tech team to provide every student with a Chromebook and even create a safe system for kids to get the devices repaired as needed, the spotty Wi-Fi service in this very low-income, heavily rural area still prevented many from going online. And although some established partners—Berea College and the local library—offered spaces for students to access Wi-Fi and work, they did not sufficiently meet the need and were too geographically distant for some. So, several local businesses stepped up to offer free Wi-Fi and allow students to study for hours in their restaurants and cafés. As a result, Deaton reports, virtually every student came to have Wi-Fi access within a five-minute walk from home.[6]

The framework of this leadership looks markedly different in the Northside Achievement Zone (NAZ) in North Minneapolis, where CEO Sondra Samuels has found her daily tasks increasingly diverted from leading her management team on academic strategies to publicly advocating for solutions to the rising incidence of extreme violence in her community. She notes that the public policy discussions on funding for the police, sensible gun laws, and "getting violence prevention folks on the streets" are "far beyond the comfort zone of nonprofit boards" such as hers. As she explains, "Given our mission of creating a culture of achievement for our children, we cannot even get to that space if we cannot keep them alive."[7] As such, Samuels works with multiple teams, including advocates and policy makers, and thus has brought NAZ leadership into new conversations and spaces, creating different types of collaboration.

On a more basic level, collaborative leadership is baked into the foundations of NAZ through the one-on-one work between family achievement coaches and families. This initiative holds parents, grandparents, and other caregivers as the key to their child's—"scholar's"—academic and life success, and it provides a range of resources to boost and empower their ability to fulfill that role. From parenting classes that might begin before a child is born to job search and career supports, and the opportunity to take on leadership roles within the initiative, NAZ families have a central seat at the table from the day they join.[8]

This ISS approach to leadership, in which the superintendent (or CEO, in the NAZ case) operates not as a central figure dispensing wisdom and orders but rather as a facilitator whose role is to bring together school leaders, educators, academic and mental health support staff, community partners, and parents, is rich in advantages felt in both good times and bad—and who is poised to enable rapid innovation and adaptation.

## COMMUNITY PARTNERS WERE INFORMED, ENGAGED, AND CRITICALLY IMPORTANT

A critical component of the successful collaboration described above was the nature and extent of the relationships that ISS communities had already established pre-pandemic, not only among schools and various governmental entities and community organizations, but also between schools and the families they serve. Both sets of relationships proved critical to the edge these districts enjoyed over most traditional public schools during the pandemic. They avoided spending precious time on needed introductions between key players and establishing ground rules for relationships, freeing partners to focus on designing and delivering actual support. As Grain Valley, Missouri, middle school teacher Nathan Perry notes, when the COVID-19 pandemic set in, "Bright Futures was working around the clock" to meet the emergency needs of their community, especially when it came to access to food. "Anybody that worked in the district that wanted to help deliver meals or deliver food" was encouraged to jump in, Perry adds.[9]

In Salem, Massachusetts, executive director of student and family support for Salem Public Schools Ellen Wingard emphasized how critical existing partnerships and the partners' deep understanding of student and community needs were. These relationships ranged from that with the local Salvation Army, a key resource for addressing significant food insecurity needs, to the North Shore Community Health Center, which not only helped provide urgent mental health supports for students and their families but also drew on its "action fund" to help families with fuel and rental assistance.[10] When Salem teachers saw something potentially troubling about a student or the student's home situation during a Zoom class, they knew whom to contact to get that student needed help.

While those relationships had already been in place in Salem, City Connects coordinator Mia Riccio says they hadn't necessarily been used to their full potential. That changed when the pandemic hit.[11] For any gaps that partners couldn't fill, City Connects coordinators could reach out to Salem Children's Charity, where Riccio's fellow coordinator Brad Maloon chaired the board.

Activities connected with the Salem Pantry during the pandemic are illustrative of the way the school district's relationships with its community partners worked. Robyn Burns, who had been executive director of the Salem Pantry for four years, had just taken on that role a month before the pandemic hit. She inherited a situation in which all the entirely volunteer organization could do was fill weekend backpacks of food for students in need. In March 2020, however, Robyn and her colleagues found themselves with no choice but to react to the developing needs of the community, schools included. She oversaw a transition from grab-and-go meals offered at school premises to home deliveries and, eventually, pop-up farmers markets that featured produce, proteins, and pantry staples.[12] Working closely with Ellen Wingard and others in the school district, Robyn and her team established a food pantry in the high school that could serve students' immediate needs for nourishment but also provide food to bring home to their families (others created a parallel "clothing connection" space to provide students with needed clothing).

The Salem YMCA's executive director Charity Lezama highlighted the perspective that she and her organization brought to the relationship with the school district: "We are all serving the same kids, and they are all our kids whether [it's] during the school day or out of school time."[13] Other entities that had participated in the Salem Children's Cabinet (see chapter 3) appeared to share this view and, as a result, the coordination of services that proved difficult, if not impossible, for other communities occurred in Salem almost as a matter of course.

And finally, in the relatively small community of Grain Valley, Missouri, with a population of approximately sixteen thousand and a school district serving approximately 4,500 students, two local churches, Road Church and the First Church of Grain Valley, have worked closely with Bright Futures USA to provide a range of services and meet the material needs of students and families.[14]

## COLLABORATIVE LEADERSHIP HELPED FACILITATE WHOLE-FAMILY, COMMUNITY-WIDE BENEFITS

Food provision is just one example of how the ISS collaborative approach helped advance strategies to support not only students but also their families throughout the pandemic. Immediate, virtually seamless food delivery—from bags loaded into car trunks to home deliveries by the Sheriff's Office of Frederick County, Virigina, and even hot meals in North Minneapolis—reduced both stress and stigma for struggling families. In Eastern Kentucky, Berea's expansion from feeding individual children to entire families, as well as adding fresh produce to bagged groceries, illustrates an ISS community's understanding of shifting to meet broader needs during a crisis.

Grain Valley's Nathan Perry recounts having one student stay on after a Google Meet classroom session had ended to confide in his teacher that, because his parents had both lost their jobs, they were working late at night to try to make ends meet.[15] As a result, the adolescent was in charge of raising his new baby sister as well as taking care of his other sister, while also trying to keep up with school, and there was not much food in the house. Concerned, Perry shared his formerly top student's stress with school administrators and leaders, who were able to connect the student with a counselor for immediate help, as well as to strategize as a school on how to implement academic policy going forward, so that students who were going through similarly turbulent periods would be supported rather than penalized when they needed extra time on assignments or other such accommodations.

ISS districts' collaborative leadership benefited families in many other ways, too. As discussed above, mental health concerns spiked among children and adults alike during the pandemic. Indeed, Berea family engagement coordinator Jenny Hobson notes that, while need had always been extensive across the nine schools she worked with, the pandemic brought in many new families who had not previously been connected with family resource centers or mental health supports and now required them. Again, with the ISS structures in place, when families came to Hobson with this range of needs, it was more a matter of connecting them with specific supports within the ISS community network than scrambling, as many other districts did, to find resources that adequately could meet the need. And as with all emergencies, response time can radically change an outcome.

Because of collaborative leadership, districts were also able to tailor resources to support parents' ability to work, which was a high priority given the disproportionate share of parents of ISS students who were likely working "essential" and other jobs that could not be performed remotely. In Salem, establishing learning labs where children could receive academic support from school professionals, along with prioritizing children whose parents had to attend work in person during fall 2020, substantially boosted parents' options as students returned to in-person schooling.

Finally, knowing how to communicate with and support families during a crisis was perhaps the most valuable, cross-cutting factor among the ISS districts. This took the shape of home visits (in driveways) in Berea, calls rather than emails to check in with parents and other caretakers in Salem, and a variety of other strategies across ISS districts. In Frederick, parent liaison Paula Johannsen was in a position, due to all of her good work with Spanish-speaking families prior to the pandemic, to be able to text with them on a regular basis.[16] In this way, she learned of issues and needs as they occurred, whether for medical services, technology support, or assistance with various governmental agencies. Paula, like other ISS coordinators and family liaisons, facilitated collaboration between these many organizations to meet the emergent and ongoing needs of students and families. Without the collaborative leadership approach that the ISS model fosters, this type of deep and efficient coordination to support communities during crises would not be nearly as effective.

## PERSISTENT CHALLENGES HIGHLIGHT BOTH THE STRENGTHS AND LIMITATIONS OF ISS

### Kids Missed Less Class, but Still a Lot, and Many Lost Real Ground (Academically, and Especially Socially and Emotionally)

Despite these efforts to support the full range of student and family needs, Salem, like other districts, struggled with chronic absenteeism as children returned to in-person learning. Ellen Wingard describes a "full-court press" to engage children and their parents in an effort to counter that gap.[17] Mia Riccio and her colleagues found that, as Salem began to bring students back in person in fall 2020, the decision many students had made in the spring to disconnect from school and not log into Zoom because school was nonmandatory was having an impact on attendance three months later. Riccio and her team therefore began to meet with students and their families to impress upon them the need to return. She recalls meeting some families at McDonald's, which was a safe and familiar place.[18]

Nathan Perry described the major social and emotional—and thus behavioral—toll that a year without being in school and lack of socializing took on students in Grain Valley (just as it did across the other districts we studied). In the middle school where he taught, this phenomenon manifested as an inability to relate normally to peers in a classroom setting, to wait for a turn to talk, and to just engage in "socially appropriate conversations."[19] His colleague, counselor Kelly Schick, noted that students seemed to lack focus, as reflected in reported problems in completing writing assignments.[20]

At the level of kindergarten, about which Perry was knowledgeable because his daughter was a student at the elementary school where his wife was also on staff, he describes real chaos, with young children never having played, worked, or collaborated in a group setting and simply not being able to do so. Many could not let go of their phones, which had come to serve as a combination babysitter and soothing mechanism during a formative year of their young lives. As he was describing what he saw in his students' difficult first months back in school, Perry also noted a major uptick in the use of energy drinks. He surmised that student sleep habits, often a major challenge among adolescents as their bodies and brains undergo substantial change, had been further disrupted by the pandemic and lack of a normal daily routine.

## Teachers Did Better Than Many Peers, but Were Still Traumatized and Burned Out

In North Minneapolis, in addition to the traumas wrought on them by the pandemic, teachers, parents, students, and others were dealing with the murder of George Floyd and the ongoing gun violence by both police and community members that hit home on a regular basis. Sondra Samuels describes how, when NAZ staff began to return to their offices in person in fall 2020, a major consideration was moving desks away from windows to avoid being caught in the crossfire as fights broke out in the streets literally on the other side of the glass.[21] And, in classrooms, teachers were helping children as young as preschoolers cope with the deaths of close friends and family members and the very real threat to their own lives that could not be denied.

Even teachers who hadn't experienced firsthand trauma faced enormous increases in stress from having to teach in new and unfamiliar ways and struggling to keep students engaged. Notwithstanding the targeted, proactive supports that PFE helped put in place, students in Appalachian Kentucky, like their peers across the country, were struggling, with many missing whole units of instruction.

As shown in this and previous chapters, while these whole-child wraparound supports are critically important, they cannot prevent or do away with an underlying emergency situation and its impacts. At the same time, educators' responses to these crisis-induced challenges reinforced the strengths of the very different approaches they have at their disposal as a result of their ISS perspective and operations. For example, Athena Deaton recalls being on the phone during March 2020 more than at any other time in her teaching career, and she describes many "really stressful" attempts to teach frightened, disconnected students on the phone.[22] Knowing that calls did not always reach students, never reached some at all, and were not enough outreach in themselves, elementary school teachers tried to bridge the gaps by visiting houses and sitting outside with whiteboards to help their students with work. So, home visits, which are a fairly common practice in ISS schools, became yet another tool in Berea-area teachers' pandemic-era kits and a way for teachers to reduce the stress and guilt they felt from being unable to provide one-on-one support.

Healthy boundaries between staff and parents also collapsed during the pandemic. Deaton describes how parents and students alike came to expect that teachers would be available at all hours for calls or texts, and that they would "get frustrated when you don't respond right away."[23] This may also, she notes, be due to a broad decline in civility in the US in recent years. Pre-COVID-19, Deaton says, angry calls from parents would get filtered through administrators, but during the pandemic, parents were present during class—they could "sit in" virtually—and Deaton soon found herself being interrupted in the middle of lessons by parents. "Some parents got more respectful, because they saw what teachers had to do, but other [student]s had parents who thought 'I could do this better.'"[24] She describes having had to mute a parent who just wanted to tell a story, or issue a "correction" to a point that, according to the parent, Deaton had taught incorrectly.

Zoom calls were already adding to teachers' stress, as was their need to work extra hard to engage and retain the attention of their students. Having to be "on" all the time, not only for their students, but also for parents, exacerbated teachers' high tendency to burn out. So, when educators returned to in-person schooling, leaders in charge of organizing professional development opportunities emphasized the importance of teachers taking time for themselves to improve their own mental and emotional well-being.

Once children started to return to school, and teachers received more attention, school leaders and others noted a high level of teacher burnout. Deaton had heard of and known many teachers who retired during 2020–2022, along with a number of substitutes who hadn't returned. This decline in staff she attributes partially to teachers who became sick during the pandemic—some of whom feared returning, others who suffered long-term health consequences—and partially to the fact that teaching now "feels like a different profession, in terms of what's expected of us, now having to adjust to the expectation of being on all the time, dealing with sleep schedules that are off, all of this!"[25]

Shontya' Washington, a very active parent in Frederick County with PTO president and elected school board member on her resume, brings a unique perspective to her observations of what occurred during and after the height of the pandemic. While acknowledging that the Frederick school system "tries to make sure we maintain healthy relationships with one another"—meaning among all of the various stakeholders in that system—she pointedly expressed concerns about the mental health of educators.[26] Washington praised teachers' heroic efforts to handle hybrid learning during the 2020–2021 school year, and she saw firsthand how the learning that occurred in classes with a smaller number of students was arguably, in some ways, a better experience for all involved than had been the case prior to the pandemic. Yet Washington also described how a great toll had been taken, suggesting that "we definitely need to drop some more oxygen masks for our teachers" so they are in a position to support those "seated" next to them, the students.[27] In her view, "oxygen masks" can take many forms and serve multiple functions, but the most critical would be an increase in behavioral specialists in each building.

## Remaining Challenges Reinforce That ISS Is Not a Solution but a Critically Needed Response to the Realities of US Crises

During the COVID-19 pandemic, the ISS communities we studied were able to leverage their collaborative leadership models, their connections with partner organizations, and their integration of parents and families into their organizational functioning to meet the challenges of the emergency head on, together. These school communities were also attuned to the social-emotional needs of students and teachers, even if they were not always able to solve the larger issues of those in need. Ellen Wingard contrasts Salem's strong performance to that of neighboring and other peer districts. Community partners and parents with whom we spoke gave her district high marks for its pandemic performance, with few if any complaints of which we became aware, while "many districts probably underserved a bunch of kids, not intentionally, but because they just couldn't do it [well]."[28]

Nonetheless, even these ISS communities confronted difficulties they could not overcome, difficulties that continue post-pandemic. Our study demonstrates how well positioned ISS communities are to contend with emergencies, both sudden and ongoing, relative to others. In fact, they not only weathered the pandemic much better than most other communities but, as chapter 5 documents, were even able to expand and grow in many cases. At the same time, the experiences of our district and school leaders, partner organizations, teachers, parents, and students also show that the ISS approach is a response to, and a strategy for addressing, but not a solution to, many of these national systemic challenges.

# 5

## ISS Communities Can Grow Stronger Through Crises

AS SCHOOLS AND DISTRICTS across the country continued to tally, and work to counter, the negative financial, academic, and organizational impacts of the COVID-19 pandemic, the integrated student supports (ISS) communities we studied were making forward progress. This is not to say that they did not also lose ground in many of the same ways as their non-ISS counterparts. Among other things, as discussed in previous chapters, many of their students fell behind both academically and socially, and teachers were burned out from teaching virtually a year or longer and, in some cases, were traumatized.

But, as also discussed, these school communities were better positioned to address the challenges brought by the pandemic. They had in place partnerships and relationships; took proactive rather than reactive approaches; and supported their students, families, and communities in a holistic manner so they ended up in a relatively stable place. As then executive director of Partners for Education (PFE) Dreama Gentry points out, "We're working in schools that are used to working with those most vulnerable [children and families], and they already have mechanisms in place. They're already aware of the vulnerabilities and assets of the population. And COVID was just another thing. It was just like the collapse of the coal industry. It was just like substance abuse."[1] As a result, they lost much less ground, and many actually had the opportunity and ability to take steps forward.

## EXPERIENCES VARIED ACROSS COMMUNITIES BUT OFTEN RESULTED IN STRENGTHENING ISS INITIATIVES

Several of the districts with which we worked described meaningful growth occurring in a variety of ways. This contrasts starkly with the holes from which many other districts continued to have to extricate themselves long after pandemic emergency conditions had lifted. This better positioning highlights another advantage conferred by the whole-child approaches and wraparound supports that distinguish ISS communities from traditional K–12 schooling models.

These ISS communities—which we studied because they are well established and robust examples of others across the country—were already growing their reach in various ways prior to the pandemic. In some respects, the emergence of COVID-19 seemed to accelerate that development rather than impede it, a counter-narrative to the general trend within US education systems of lost academic ground and inadequate resources.

## PARTNERS FOR RURAL IMPACT

Based at Berea College, Kentucky, PFE grew in several respects during the COVID-19 pandemic and has continued to do so in its aftermath. In January 2022, it was renamed Partners for Rural Impact (PRI) and became an independent nonprofit entity, separating from Berea College where it had been housed for over fifty years. The move was part of the organization's evolution into a leadership role as a rural ISS and, specifically, community school model. As Dreama Gentry describes, "This is a graduation party, not a messy divorce. We just got so big. Our budget is the same as the College's instructional budget, and it just got to the point of, okay, you really do need to be on your own."[2] PRI's journey in recent years illustrates both the power of this model and the high and growing level of unmet need:

> While PRI began by serving a single county, it now supports young people and their communities in 31 counties in Appalachian Kentucky. . . . As it moves forward, PRI will expand its cradle-to-career model in Kentucky. Providing wrap-around services to meet students' social and emotional needs has a demonstrated impact on educational outcomes. *Ultimately, the goal is to expand educational opportunities in all of rural America.* PRI's leadership will reach beyond Appalachia to develop and nurture the relationships needed to create a broad-based, diverse set of partners dedicated to ensuring all rural students succeed.[3]

Since the receipt of its first federal grant to support a Full-Service Community School (FSCS) program, PRI has grown into a learning and advocacy hub, advancing the adoption and implementation of FSCS programs in rural communities across the country.[4] In January 2023, for example, Gentry joined a panel at a Brookings Institution event to announce the launch of a set of new resources being produced by the Community Schools Forward Task Force, highlighting the unique strategies PRI is helping rural communities to adopt in order to implement effective community-school approaches.[5]

The growth of its leadership team from three to seven—with four new vice presidents—over the 2022–2023 school year illustrates this expansion and points to the potential for much greater impact in the years to come. A new vice president for capacity-building oversees several bodies of work, including civic infrastructure, which is "helping communities in places as diverse as Washington State, Missouri, and Appalachia build and align partnerships."[6] She also has helped spearhead the expansion of PRI's family engagement team, which launched statewide family engagement grants in Arkansas, in partnership with Save the Children, and New Hampshire, with Campus Compact, building on the work it has been doing in Eastern Kentucky. In addition to Save the Children, PRI is strengthening its work with StriveTogether, an organization with which it has long had both shared interests and practical ties. Place-based partnership work is likewise expanding rapidly under the leadership of another new vice president, starting with foundations invested in rural communities in East Texas and Mexico, Missouri. This substantial growth during and in the immediate aftermath of the pandemic illustrates the strength and resilience of the ISS approach, and the stark contrast it makes with narrower, less collaborative and holistic education structures.

This work involves a combination of capacity-building, research on what works in rural settings, and advancing a rural agenda at the national level to complement this on-the-ground work. These wide-ranging efforts came together under a single umbrella at PRI's inaugural Rural Summit in 2024, which took place in upstate New York. Finally, Associate Vice President of Strategic Communications (now Senior Vice President) J. Morgan reports that "we've recently developed an instructional design team that is codifying our best practices, including our model for rural community schools."[7] In resource-poor but relationship-rich communities like Berea, these practices include educating, empowering, and recruiting local parents as organizers and trainers for other parents, like mother and (now) family engagement specialist Sue Christian. Morgan notes, too, that PRI will be exploring other rural "regions of persistent poverty" where the new organization might open offices to be staffed by local leaders, as it has done in Appalachia. These expansions all reflect and advance Gentry's ambitious vision for PRI, community schools, and rural education more broadly, and PRI's view that lifting up communities requires leaders who know those communities best.

Even as this national growth has transpired, on the local front, PRI has leveraged its series of FSCS grants, as described above, to further expand services in eight counties.[8] President and CEO Gentry points to the organization's strategic use of these grants to better coordinate key services for students and families in relevant communities during the pandemic, an effort that our interviewees in these schools reflected in their perceptions of stronger, smoother collaboration and communication. (This advantage contrasts with the frustration that others working in non-FSCS schools in the area expressed regarding problematic communication and collaboration between PRI and the school districts.)

## NORTHSIDE ACHIEVEMENT ZONE

Berea is not the only ISS community to expand its services during the pandemic. The Northside Achievement Zone (NAZ), which, in addition to serving student "scholars" from preK to college-bound, supports five early childhood centers in North Minneapolis and has built into its three-year strategic plan doula and home visiting services for expecting mothers.[9] These new supports will complement a robust early childhood strategy that already includes high-quality early education and parenting classes for mothers and fathers of young children. Indeed, in addition to College-Bound Babies, College-Bound Scholars, a "Proud Pop" class specifically for Black fathers, and a Foundations class for parents, NAZ has introduced a Youth Foundations class that enables parents and their scholars to gain valuable life skills and tools for self-empowerment together.[10] NAZ parent Angelina Courtney discusses how beneficial the class has been for her and her son: "[They] really covered it all. Like talking about nutrition, and how proper nutrition affects your body, and how the foods we eat, how they show up in our behaviors, and the way we think.... That was helpful for me as a parent to show my kids like, 'Hey, it's not just mom being mean' and that the stuff really does matter."[11]

Angelina emphasized how the classes, the family achievement coaches, and NAZ as an overall organization have been a great source of support for her and her four children, especially during the pandemic. While COVID-19 was raging and since, NAZ doubled the number of family achievement coaches it deploys in schools, from around a dozen at the start of the pandemic to twenty-five by summer 2023.[12] Perhaps an even bigger sign of its increasing traction and centrality in the community, the decade-old NAZ initiative expanded to a new building for operations in April 2022, though for a terrible reason it wished were not the case: as discussed in chapter 4, there was so much gun violence taking place right around the old building, with windows constantly getting shot out, staff could not safely work there. NAZ CEO Sondra Samuels said her staff were "dealing with enough" already and should not have to worry about their personal safety at work.[13]

The new building is not the only NAZ innovation to emerge in response to the increasing violence. Samuels shared stories of multiple students being killed in gang-related gun violence, and how families and teachers have been traumatized by these sudden deaths, but also the beautiful memorials NAZ continues to create for these kids.[14] NAZ's related focus on expanding wellness initiatives took place both at the district level and at the school level. For instance, at Ascension Catholic School, one of the schools that is part of NAZ, Principal Benito Matias points to the breathing techniques and yoga sessions that the school instituted with support from NAZ. They never would have considered such actions were it not for the needs they saw during the pandemic, he says, but they have proven to be powerfully beneficial, giving students new, healthy ways to express and regulate their emotions, and he will likely make them an ongoing addition to the school's offerings.[15]

While most of the ISS communities we studied are located in areas of high poverty and have many related challenges, we believe it is important to recognize the specifics of each context and the reality that serving areas of high need means grappling with those needs in real time. As discussed, these needs have long existed in North Minneapolis, but the brutal combination of the pandemic and George Floyd's murder elevated them in unique respects. As an exemplar ISS community, NAZ responded by supporting its people in deep and holistic ways.

## CITY CONNECTS

Appalachian Kentucky is not the only ISS area to see a leadership expansion in recent years. The Mary E. Walsh Center for Thriving Children at Boston College, which launched and houses the City Connects program, also saw major recent growth. Longtime head Mary E. Walsh, who is the founding director of the center and remains a senior fellow, was succeeded in September 2023 as executive director by Eric Dearing, with Claire Foley continuing as associate director. Both Dearing and Foley have long been involved in the work of the center and of City Connects; their leadership roles reflect the evolution of City Connects with respect to both on-the-ground work and enhanced work in research and practical guidance.

Similar to practices in NAZ, Salem Public Schools also began to diversify its ISS programming during the pandemic. City Connects middle school coordinator Mia Riccio says that the pandemic strengthened and expanded the organization's capacity to support students and their families:

In a lot of ways [my role as coordinator is] the same. But I think in a lot of ways ... we've just gotten better at what we're doing right. We know of more community organizations that can support. We're thinking about things in a more systematic way so that we're able to target more students through a tiered approach. I think we've just honed our skills. . . . I think the heartache that the pandemic put everyone through . . . allowed us space to think about how we wanted to do things differently.[16]

Riccio specifically pointed to an organization that a teacher at the Carlton Innovation School (grades K–5) engaged during the pandemic. Talewise comes into the school and provides interactive lessons that combine stories and science experiments that the students take part in conducting.[17] These types of interdisciplinary lessons seemed to be especially effective during the pandemic when engagement strategies were needed even more than usual.

Ellen Wingard, executive director of student and family support services at Salem Public Schools, says teachers have really grown; having more detailed windows into kids' lives has enabled them to better support their students.[18] Teachers who live in neighboring towns began to "choice" (opt) their kids into Salem schools post-pandemic, after seeing the positive impact of the comprehensive supports approach. Community stakeholders also gave very positive feedback; in a stark contrast to how other non-ISS communities were perceived as performing during the pandemic, Salem received substantial praise and virtually no complaints of which we are aware.

From the perspective of one of the school district's key partners, Robyn Burns, and the Salem Pantry she heads, the evolution in how the two organizations related to each other during the pandemic has led to more opportunities to improve food security. The Salem Pantry always analyzes data about how its services are being used, and to the extent the school district can share its own data about, for example, how students are making use of the high school pantry, more targeted services can be provided to reduce the impacts of hunger on students' educational experiences. Burns hopes to be able to further collaborate with Salem Public Schools to strengthen the data sharing, among other possible advances.

## BRIGHT FUTURES IN FREDERICK COUNTY PUBLIC SCHOOLS

In Frederick County Public Schools (FCPS), practices that developed during the pandemic have had a lasting positive effect as all stakeholders have continued to adapt to the current realities of the K–12 education world. Mario Giamporcaro, then a guidance counselor at Frederick County Middle School, offers a unique perspective on the value of Frederick's model. He moved from a position in another well-regarded school district to employment at FCPS in 2020, right in the midst of the pandemic. He noted how a very effective three-way communication system had been established among the middle school teachers, the counselors, and the Bright Futures coordinator so that when anyone identified a problem with students or their families, he or she would notify the others to ensure a coordinated response.[19]

He also highlighted that, in a far-flung district in which some families live distant from their children's schools, during the height of the pandemic parents could drive to a relatively convenient parking lot where school staff would venture out among the cars to work with the parents and family members on how to use Chromebooks and Wi-Fi hotspots so they could more effectively support their children at home. That kind of interaction, along with a number of other kinds between FCPS staff and families, generated a great deal of trust that paid dividends. Students started coming in to talk to Giamporcaro more regularly and freely about topics that extend beyond classroom concerns, and he began seeing parents being more invested in their children's education and the schools: "In their child's education, they want them to succeed so now they're trying to learn more about [technology], you know some parents have never even touched technology so it's really cool to see that."[20]

The experience of the Frederick schools has also heavily informed the "Portrait of a Graduate" initiative, part of the district's Inspire 2025 strategic plan. This portrait, which was developed by a group of parents, students, business/community leaders, and school staff, aims to represent competencies needed for students to be successful and "life ready." Social and cultural empathy is highlighted as one of those competencies, and this has emerged virtually everywhere in the United States as a top priority in K–12 schools.[21]

## BRIGHT FUTURES IN GRAIN VALLEY, MISSOURI

Grain Valley middle school history teacher Nathan Perry feels that the unique challenges of the pandemic strengthened bonds not only among teachers at his school, but also across the district as a whole. Having gone into the pandemic with new school leadership and substantial turnover, and thus several new teachers, he and his peers built on that new foundation to forge strong relationships that met the moment's unique needs: "We really have developed, I would say, a need and a desire to care for each other, to help each other out . . . with this sub shortage, like today, I had to leave school right after the first hour because my kid was sick. And I told my boss that I really needed to go, and he said, 'Don't even hesitate, just go, we'll get it figured out.' No other sub has filled my position, but other teachers have."[22]

With ISS at the ready, these schools were able to be more flexible when teachers, administrators, and staff needed to attend to unexpected needs brought on by the crisis. As a result, as Perry's experience helps to demonstrate, educators and administrators in ISS districts were often better positioned to adapt from previous norms to meet the new challenges introduced by the pandemic, and thus more likely to survive, and even grow, rather than to fall behind.

Emerging from the pandemic, certain Grain Valley partnerships that were nascent as the pandemic began have gotten stronger. An example of this is the partnership between the schools and the local Road Church and its senior pastor, Dr. Dale Smith. In 2018, Smith had approached Grain Valley North Middle School to offer the church's support for whatever might be needed. The relationship had just gotten started in 2020, but during and in the aftermath of the pandemic, it evolved to the point that the church came to dedicate a specific line item in its budget for the middle school.

The church's understanding of both student and staff needs is also evident in how those funds are spent. Pastor Smith has taken such seemingly small actions as providing snacks for students during Missouri state assessment testing; showing support for faculty and staff by supplying treats for them on various special occasions; and providing gift cards for students in need at Christmas. Grain Valley North Middle School counselor Kelly Schick, who is the primary contact for the pastor and the school's relationship with the church, has become such a regular presence that, as Smith notes, "If I don't hear from her after so many weeks or months . . . I'll reach out to her to see if there is a need."[23] The church also has a relationship with a bigger network, the Community Services League, and thus can bring those resources to bear as appropriate.

## ACROSS ISS COMMUNITIES, GROWTH INCLUDED BETTER ALIGNMENT BETWEEN ACADEMIC AND SOCIAL-EMOTIONAL SUPPORTS

While wraparound supports had long been understood by many to be a critical component enabling effective instruction and meaningful learning, educators and others we spoke to reported that the pandemic brought home the reality that these components are two sides of the same coin, rather than separate, complementary ones.

In Berea, Dreama Gentry optimistically describes an era in which we are "overcoming the backlash of accountability," with children's social and emotional well-being shifting from being chiefly the responsibility of a few staff to having every person in a school thinking of both academics and students' emotional health. The next phase, she says, is developing meaningful metrics that capture both, rather than viewing the latter as one lever to improve traditional academic achievement.[24]

Grain Valley's Nathan Perry says that while Bright Futures had been a central presence in that community for several years preceding the pandemic, the COVID-19 emergency brought home certain recognitions. For example, there was a newfound realization that not only do teachers need to focus on their students' academic needs, they also need to pay attention to a child who may not have dental care or eyeglasses, and thus cannot focus due to pain or inability to see.[25] Improving this balance, in turn, strengthens teachers' relationships with both students and the community partners who help meet those needs. Additionally, Counselor Kelly Schick highlighted the steps that Grain Valley North Middle School took to provide school-based mental health services once the heightened need for them was recognized. Her team partnered with two outside service providers, one of which accepted Medicaid and another that took private insurance. Because of the demand, the school actually built a small room inside a larger conference room outside Schick's office to accommodate the service providers.[26]

In Minneapolis, the deep, extensive network of partnerships that NAZ has cultivated over the past decade similarly enabled growth, rather than retraction, during the pandemic, thanks in part to the collaborative leadership structure it developed. At Ascension Catholic School, Principal Matias describes staff working together to evolve their system for needs assessment and tracking of supports to meet the new realities brought about by the pandemic. They created a shared Google Sheet with every scholar's name, organized by grade, enabling teachers to track every single interaction with families in a shared space. That dynamic, he said, provided teachers a unique window into their students' homes, prompting teachers to express to him "a stronger sense of connection [with families] and more fluid and more organic communication."[27] This approach by a NAZ school, which is consistent with that of City Connects districts such as Salem, illustrates the close connection between academic and nonacademic needs that ISS communities quickly recognized and acted on during the pandemic.

---

## THE POWERFUL IMPACT OF ISS COMMUNITIES

These ISS communities' uniquely expansive approaches to education policy and practice, and their resulting capacity to leverage broad networks of resources and relationships during the pandemic, have also produced a few success stories that sound more like fairytales than reality. But they are very real, and they provide powerful evidence that incredible turnarounds are possible when the right leadership, philosophy, and structures are in place. They also remind us all of the importance of not letting stereotypes cloud our judgment regarding what is possible.

### Frederick County Public Schools

In a decade in which the very serious problems caused by having police officers work in schools—as school resource officers (SROs)—have become increasingly clear around the United States, the Frederick County Sheriff's Office, in close collaboration with the school district and Bright Futures, showcases what could be possible if we flipped the SRO model on its head.[28] When we heard the following words from Sergeant Travis Mitchell—"I absolutely love the schools and what we do, and the connections that we have with these scholars"—we were alerted to a very special phenomenon.[29]

Over the past several years, the local Sheriff's Office joined a growing group of district-area businesses, nonprofits, and governmental agencies engaged with FCPS through Bright Futures. The officers did not, however, see their primary role as enforcing discipline in schools or removing students who were behaving badly—Sergeant Mitchell seemed almost surprised at that suggestion during an interview. Rather, like the district's various other partners, they approached school leadership with questions about how they could best help with the communal effort—that is, what was the Sheriff's Office uniquely positioned to contribute?

The answer has turned out to be multifaceted, very surprising, and continually evolving. Early on, teachers, counselors, and social workers reported a need for more "safe adults" to serve as lunch buddies for younger students—to come into the schools at lunchtime to eat with kindergartners and first and second graders, chat about what's going on in school and out of school, and be available as a sounding board and mentor. The Sheriff's Office saw this as a perfect match—deputies had flexible schedules that enabled this weekly interaction, and building these relationships would foster trust between children and law enforcement, reinforcing the latter's role as a resource for schools, families, and the community at large.

This relationship grew over the subsequent years into a powerful and central part of the Bright Futures Frederick/Winchester initiative. It has manifested itself in ways ranging from having officers raising money for, and operating, annual summer camps for middle school students to serving on the Bright Futures board, as Sergeant Mitchell has done. The Sheriff's Office also has organized a Community Safety Fair which, in addition to introducing families to emergency apparatus and personnel, offered an opportunity to provide

FIGURE 5.1  The Frederick County Sheriff on roller skates at elementary school. Photograph courtesy of Jason Cornwell.

information about Bright Futures' services. The relationship leads to unique scenes, such as when colleagues of Sergeant Mitchell joined an elementary school physical education class on roller skates in January 2023 (figure 5.1).[30]

Given these well-established relationships, the apparent trust students and schools developed for the sheriff's deputies, and the deputies' increasing sense that the schools were an integral component of their community safety responsibilities, it perhaps was unsurprising that deputies were among the first to step up to fill gaps that emerged in the early days of the pandemic. As Sergeant Mitchell notes, when schools closed down and public health restrictions prevented school personnel and others from coming into contact with families, the Sheriff's Office could, and did, receive and organize items for redistribution and deliver food to families. The trusting relationships also meant they could use those opportunities to make other visits to homes to check in on students, refer them to resources, and serve as crucial liaisons between those families and school leadership. Moreover, it was not only the SROs who engaged, but also other deputies in the Sheriff's Office—for example, when officers became aware that a student had been sleeping on the floor for lack of a bed, deputies procured and brought one to the student's house.[31]

## Northside Achievement Zone

Angelina Courtney grew up in North Minneapolis with the kinds of big dreams and limited opportunities typical of many of her friends, family members, and neighbors. She wanted a good job that would lead to a stable career; happy, healthy, thriving children; and a home of her own in a safe place where her children would succeed. By her mid-twenties, however, that vision looked increasingly out of reach. Angelina had her first child, a daughter, when she was seventeen, and her second, a son, when she was twenty-one. And although she was working hard—leveraging scholarships to study for a two-year degree and securing affordable housing outside the city—the high cost of child care, long commutes from the family's small apartment, and lack of resources for her son, who needed additional educational supports beyond the traditional classroom, posed major barriers.[32]

Then, in 2019, Angelina joined NAZ. She had first heard of the organization in 2010, when her son was born, but the constant demands of staying afloat had made engaging too hard. Joining turned out to be life changing. Right from the start, Angelina's family achievement coach, Tatika Taylor, started to help turn things around. One of the first concerns Angelina conveyed was that her academic support was about to disappear; it had taken her too long to complete the credits required to get her degree, and she could not knock out all three of the remaining courses to graduate on time. "Yes, Tatika said, "you can, and you will. Your children—all four of them—need to see you walk across that stage, and I will be there with them cheering you on. This is the first goal you need to set for yourself."

Not long after that goal was realized with a graduation both women describe as beautiful and powerful, Angelina called Tatika to ask if she could come with her to check out a house she was considering buying. The apartment her family was then living in was owned by Angelina's boss, and he had been using it as leverage to keep her in a job that did not pay enough and that did not let her showcase her talents or skills. When Tatika walked through the door of the duplex, Angelina proudly informed her coach that she had just bought it—goal number two in pursuit of her dream.

Angelina went on to enroll herself and her children in NAZ's Family Academy courses, which have helped her improve both how she treats herself and how she interacts with her children, mirroring her new belief in her ability to control and shape her life. The process has been transformative, Angelina says, giving her "a sense of understanding and community," and allowing her to draw strength from "the fact that people believe in the community and in me as a mother, as a woman, as a Black woman."[33] Recently, as noted above, she participated in the dual-generation Foundations class—which had previously been for adults only—with her older son, Christian, who was among the pioneers of the new Youth Foundations version.

When we spoke to her in June 2023, Angelina was preparing for a big move. She had recently landed a job with Google—a huge step up that she credits in large part to the self-confidence and empowerment developed through her collaboration with NAZ, one-on-one work with Tatika, and, more recently, joining the Parent Advisory Board, through which she helped to inform NAZ practice and policy. Her four children, then aged sixteen, thirteen, eight, and five years old, would be continuing their education in Columbus, Ohio, where Angelina intends to build a new community for her family and, she says, maybe even start the first NAZ outpost.[34]

## LESSONS LEARNED

As these examples illustrate, communities that have been preparing for crises, tackling them head on, and having built the resources and relationships needed to do so, not only weathered the pandemic better than their less prepared counterparts, but also were often able to build upon the strong foundations they had laid to continue making progress while many others lost substantial ground. Given the growing number and types of emergencies facing our communities, these examples provide powerful lessons that we can, and need to, learn from and adapt to particular situations.

## 1. Every Challenge Also Presents New Opportunities

Outside of the education policy world, this may just be a cliché, but inside of it, the lesson has largely gone unappreciated. As school reform efforts over recent decades illustrate, too often, those making key decisions have viewed the challenges schools face as *obstacles*—increasingly, obstacles that cannot be overcome—rather than as *opportunities* to try new strategies and learn new approaches.

These ISS communities have faced schools' challenges head on and developed a broad range of creative strategies to improve education not just for their students with the highest needs, but for *all* their students. And the value of this approach was on full display during the COVID-19 pandemic. As described in this chapter, some of the new tactics that schools adopted turned out to have unanticipated benefits. The teacher preparation days that some districts initiated during the pandemic were so helpful that they began to explore options to preserve the practice in post-pandemic contexts. And Zoom classes helped some shyer students feel more comfortable participating in class, so teachers in those classes planned to work with their school leaders to identify ways to sustain that momentum—perhaps by finding a way to secure small-group opportunities for those who need them—while returning as many students as possible to full-time, in-person learning.

This lesson has broad application across the crises schools face. Rather than racing to install metal detectors when gun violence rates rise, schools should boost mental and emotional health resources for their students, including adopting peer mediation and other restorative justice strategies, as eastern Appalachian schools in the Berea region have done.

## 2. Make Parents True Partners

This is another piece of common education policy wisdom that has long been heavy on the talk and light on the walk. However, ISS communities understand that meaningfully engaging parents requires empowering them and nurturing relationships over time by building trust. Empowering parents in this way also creates a virtuous cycle. Building committees and boards of engaged, informed parents who understand firsthand the powerful benefits of ISS approaches not only strengthens schools in a variety of ways in the immediate (and longer) term, but it can also help avert the leadership churn and repeated strategic change-of-direction that all too often derails school improvement efforts.

And, as Angelina Courtney in North Minneapolis and Sue Christian in Berea, among others, demonstrate, as parents move into new spaces and communities, they bring with them the seeds to create new ISS schools and districts and start making this community-centered, whole-child approach to K–12 education the norm, rather than an exception.

# 6

# ISS Schools' Roles in Community Resilience and Economic Stabilization

WHILE MANY AMERICANS TEND to picture K–12 schools as simply providing instruction and education, in reality they do much more: these schools are key components of community prosperity and well-being and critical to the social fabric. Particularly at times when other institutions, service providers, and social systems are overextended or even closed, such as during recessions and natural disasters, schools often supplement or even substitute for them. And in addition to the myriad important social roles they play, public schools can also act as economic stabilizers, especially for smaller and more disadvantaged communities, and particularly during economic downturns.[1]

Because they are part of the public rather than the private sector, we tend not to view such schools in this light, but public schools constitute a large economic sector, employing a substantial share of the American workforce.[2] In times when other community employers—supermarkets, corporate offices, barber shops, and warehouses—cut back or close, the teachers, aides, nurses, librarians, and other staff employed by our public

schools become even more critical to sustaining a community's economic infrastructure, continuing to pour money into the local economy
when it is needed most.

These are also times, however, when such schools are most likely
to suffer cuts, and to need more federal support. As Sylvia Allegretto,
Emma Garcia, and Elaine Weiss note in their 2022 report for the Economic Policy Institute, the targeted funding directed to schools in the
aftermath of the Great Recession of 2008 as part of the American Recovery and Reinvestment Act largely achieved its goal of shielding schools,
especially high-poverty schools, from deep state- and local-based budget
cuts. Similar to the formula supporting Unemployment Insurance and
the Supplemental Nutrition Assistance Program (SNAP, formerly the
Food Stamp Program), the authors argue that building such funding into
federal allocations for public education could do much more, especially
during and in the aftermath of economic downturns, to provide a cush-
ion to the economy as a whole:

> [Such] countercyclical investments would keep the public educa-
> tion workforce employed. The teachers, nurses, counselors, librar-
> ians, bus drivers, cafeteria workers, and others who work in public
> schools made up 53.2% of all state and local public-sector workers in
> 2019—accounting for nearly 7.0% of total U.S. employment. School
> staff are also family and community members whose spending ripples
> through their local economies (known as the multiplier effect).[3]

Viewed from a different angle, there is evidence that ISS schools in
particular provide an important economic benefit to their communities.
These schools' unique approach of bringing together all of a community's
actors that work with children to collaborate is not only educationally
smart and productive, but also economically efficient. For example,
situating Boys & Girls Club activities and counseling sessions in school
buildings may reduce both parents' and students' logistical challenges
and improve those organizations' bottom lines. In fact, Jennifer Vey and

Juanita Morales asserted in a 2022 Brookings Institution brief that local government leaders should see the integration of various publicly supported nonprofit organizations with community schools not as an ask for new money, but rather as a more efficient repurposing of existing resources.[4]

Other research indicates that, in the end, both students and the local economy benefit. An illustrative case study by the Finance Project and the Children's Aid Society found that attendance in community schools can result in higher earnings for students who graduate from high school and, importantly, that community schools have a positive long-term impact on municipal budgets through the reduced use of publicly financed social services when those students reach adulthood.[5]

## SCHOOLS BOOST COMMUNITY RESILIENCE

In addition to playing a potentially valuable role in economic stabilization, schools that provide ISS are integral to advancing community resilience. We have seen this time and again in our research and have included a number of examples in this book. Creating community resilience can be challenging and the phenomenon is complex. In a systematic literature review, researchers outlined the key ingredients common across multiple studies of the concept:

- local knowledge
- community networks and relationships
- communication
- health within the community
- governance/leadership
- community resources
- emergency preparedness
- economic investment
- positive mental outlook[6]

These core elements are seen as crucial to providing critical support and structure for communities faced with emergency situations such as pandemics, natural disasters, or human tragedies. According to disaster preparedness literature, in communities in which these elements are present before an emergency develops, the probability of the community maintaining itself and the speed with which it does so—and, ultimately, recovers—often improves.[7]

It is well recognized that in terms of emergency preparedness, schools frequently act as community shelters, offering safety from extreme weather events or infrastructure failures. Across the tornado-prone US South, school gymnasiums may be the safest place to weather a bad storm and are often the only space that can house families who lose their homes. As a 2017 article from the National Education Association's news outlet illustrates, public schools and school staff in Houston, Texas, and Miami, Florida, provided shelter and comfort to thousands of displaced families in the back-to-back 2017 "monster" Hurricanes Harvey and Irma:

> Across Florida, counties have agreements with their school districts to use their school buildings as evacuation shelters during hurricanes. The reasons are clear—public schools are in every community; they are safe, public spaces that are solidly built, and officials know how many people they can hold. What's more, school staff are always at the ready to help their students, families and community members. It's at the heart of what they do every day.[8]

This sense of schools as especially safe spaces may be partly responsible for a well-known case of false optimism in the 1950s, when they were depicted as places of safety in the event of a nuclear attack, so long as students and teachers took cover under desks!

These examples help illustrate that, as a country, we have actually long believed that schools enhance resilience and help to future-proof our communities. Beyond US borders, the United Nations has highlighted schools as an important mitigating factor in disaster response for communities.[9] In 2020, researchers from Harvard's Edmond J. Safra Center for Ethics emphasized that schools, specifically, are "sites and sources of community resilience in five distinct ways: they distribute social welfare services, promote human development, care for children, provide stable employment, and strengthen democratic solidarity."[10] Schools provide the foundations for a combination of social, economic, and civic development and should thus be widely recognized as cornerstones of community resilience.

While traditional schools also can and do increase community resilience, we argue that schools providing ISS are particularly key to any such effort. Interviews with people working in the ISS communities discussed in this book make clear how the ISS approach contributed to community resilience not only during the pandemic but also prior to its onset, and how it continues to do so as we face (and will continue to face) other ongoing emergencies. More specifically, our ISS communities have been integral to bolstering community resilience by providing resources to improve nutrition, physical and mental health, housing stability, and employment in response to and independently of crises. We examine this in more depth below.

## FEEDING COMMUNITIES

In communities in which hunger and poor nutrition are endemic, schools that actively seek to support their students and families through the provision of food are playing an important role in ensuring those communities' resilience. While many schools found themselves suddenly serving as centers of food distribution during the pandemic, and many stepped up and performed admirably, few coordinated in the way ISS schools in our sample were able to do.

Because of their strong ties to the communities in which they are located, schools offering ISS can serve as information hubs and clearinghouses for resources. This is true even in our age of easy electronic linkages. More than most traditional public schools, ISS schools have built trusting relationships with their respective communities over time and are therefore viewed as reliable and credible.

By virtue of their different partnerships, ISS schools can be facilitators of broader networks of support that go beyond the school community. In Massachusetts, the evolution of the work of the Salem Pantry under Robyn Burns helps to illustrate this point. In tracing for us the relationship of her organization (prior to her time with the Pantry) to Salem Public Schools, Burns noted how the Pantry evolved from having a relatively small volunteer effort that was able to provide enough food items to fill 150–200 student backpacks per week to recognizing that, by working with the YMCA, it could help alleviate the summer food crisis that affects the predominantly low-income community of Salem when schools are not open to provide daily meals.[11]

In the case of Frederick County Public Schools (FCPS) in Virginia, the food operations overseen by Bright Futures USA were well known and appreciated by the community prior to COVID-19. But during the height of the pandemic, local food banks that could not remain open contacted the Bright Futures coordinator, Nancy Mango, to see if the school district could take the lead in meeting the needs of people who depended on them and, of course, the schools obliged to the extent possible. In fact, the Bright Futures Frederick/Winchester food distribution effort extended beyond traditional recipients of school meals and support. Because Bright Futures is so well integrated into the social service support system of the Frederick/Winchester area, as both FCPS and outside entities identified unmet needs, Mango and her team did not stop to worry—in that critical moment—about whether a potential recipient of food help was associated with the schools or was an unaffiliated county resident. If the schools had the capacity to provide assistance, they did so.[12]

While perhaps not the most prominent benefit, this aspect of community resilience also boosts the local economy in multiple ways. When more children eat regular, nutritious meals, not only do they perform better and achieve more in school and require fewer costly remedial and special education services, they are also less likely to end up in counseling offices and in local emergency rooms, another burden to local economies.[13] This is also true of their parents, who, in addition to being healthier and less reliant on expensive publicly funded health care, are in a better position to obtain employment and able to work more productively on the job.

## MAINTAINING COMMUNITY PHYSICAL AND MENTAL HEALTH

Another way in which ISS schools are key to community resilience is the role they play in maintaining both the physical and mental health of youth and their families. While traditional K–12 schools primarily, and sometimes solely, focus on serving the students of record, ISS schools often include the entire household in their wellness strategies. In an ISS community, family members of all ages, from newborns to elders, are considered. In Minneapolis, the Northside Achievement Zone (NAZ)'s decision to expand its intensive Foundations classes during the pandemic to include youth along with their parents provides just one example of the whole-family, whole-community wellness endeavors advanced by ISS communities. Research shows that a child's entire family ecosystem has an influence on his/her health and well-being—and, therefore, the ability to learn and achieve in school.[14]

In Salem, recognizing the heightened challenges students faced in the aftermath of COVID-19, the school district decided to expand beyond the existing network of school adjustment counselors and create a comprehensive mental health framework. Starting in fall 2022, Salem planned for universal mental health screening and universal social-emotional learning screening for all students, a critical support not only for a well-functioning school environment but also for the broader community.[15] And, like the other school districts we studied, Salem Public Schools was already part of a well-established network of service providers in the community, so that when COVID-19 prevented various community mental health providers from meeting with clients in person, Salem's ISS community played a key role in helping to ensure that families were able to access telehealth sessions.

At a time when mental health supports are increasingly stretched thin and difficult to obtain in many communities, building student and family well-being into education policy and practice also makes economic sense, especially because people in low-income households often suffer more, may experience more severe mental health problems, and are much less likely to be able to access care. Since services are often integrated into the funding and logistics frameworks of the ISS system, mental health care providers can often provide their support at a lower cost to students and families in need. Perhaps most crucial, increased support for preventive care and crisis aversion helps reduce some of the most costly, longest-term, and often least effective forms of mental and emotional care.[16]

## HOUSING COMMUNITIES

Among the myriad national crises exposed and exacerbated by the pandemic, lack of affordable housing, evictions, and homelessness stand out. And here, too, ISS communities have been working to address a broader societal emergency and improve family and community resilience. For many years, NAZ has included as a core objective helping families secure stable, affordable, and safe housing. During the COVID-19 emergency, families in Minneapolis could access certain government-provided emergency relief to help them with housing costs. But with the end of that funding, NAZ recognized that if it was going to help its families work their way out of poverty and enable their young scholars to take advantage of educational opportunities, it would have to help procure rental assistance for the families. With an extensive network to draw on, NAZ was able to turn to its housing partners to construct a rental stability program.[17]

In each of the ISS communities we studied, to varying extents, challenges around housing have continued to surface as impediments to family and student success. Whether it was the ability of the Frederick County Sheriff's Office to step in during the pandemic and provide a mattress to a student who school leaders and staff had learned was sleeping on the floor at home, or other districts being able to use their deep knowledge of families' housing needs to direct them to appropriate community resources, ISS communities have been able to make a difference in addressing issues related to both poor-quality housing and housing instability.[18]

As rapidly intensifying crises around housing unaffordability and homelessness across the country demonstrate, preventing such emergencies also leads to substantial cost savings for the public. Unhoused students and their families are disproportionately likely to suffer health problems that, in turn, cost the community more in taxpayer-funded care. Providing emergency housing in shelters or even hotels is inevitably much more costly and, again, logistically challenging, than taking steps to prevent a family from becoming evicted or homeless.[19]

Under the McKinney-Vento Homeless Assistance Act, which Congress reauthorized in 2015 as part of the passage of the Every Student Succeeds Act, students experiencing homelessness are eligible for a range of special supports. While critically important for these vulnerable students, these resources can be very expensive and practically difficult for districts to implement, and, of course, they do not fully compensate for the damage done by being homeless, so reducing the number of students who require such supports is the far better option.[20]

## EMPLOYING COMMUNITIES

ISS schools and districts often view family members as potential future employees, a particular advantage in areas that have been hit by industrial shifts, mass layoffs, addiction, incarceration, and other drivers of chronic joblessness. In Appalachian Kentucky, for example, Partners for Rural Impact seeks not only to engage families that have historically been left out of their children's education, but also to empower them to take leading roles in school policy and practice. Many current family engagement coordinators were, just a few years ago, parents who came reluctantly to meetings about becoming more engaged. One such specialist, Sue Christian, describes her own prior feelings of inadequacy as a parent; now she recruits her peers to join the next generation of ISS community leaders, advancing new policies based on personal experiences with the schools and their children.[21]

In NAZ, many family achievement coaches are community members, and some are former and/or current NAZ families who may themselves have previously received support from coaches. Like the family engagement coordinators in the Berea region, these coaches' long-standing, firsthand experiences in the community, including their understanding of both the deep ties families have to the neighborhood and each other, and the complex challenges these families face in raising children who will be college- and career-ready, offer a powerful advantage.

This approach to expanding the NAZ and Berea workforces from within illustrates ISS schools' capacity to boost both communities' economic well-being and their resilience. Like other aspects of ISS, these efforts transform a potential liability—parents who have little formal education and are viewed by employers (and often by school leaders) as "low-skilled"—into a valuable asset. In doing so, ISS communities expand the local labor market while simultaneously lifting those trapped at the bottom of it.

## CONNECTING COMMUNITIES

A community is most resilient when the various institutions and sectors that comprise it—education, business, religious, governmental, and more—are all functioning at optimal levels and, most importantly, are working together effectively. A school providing ISS is often interacting with all these other entities and can serve as a "connector" among them. Indeed, a recurring theme from our interviews is the unique leadership and hub role schools (and other ISS agencies) serve; absent their ISS approaches, many of these entities would rarely even interact with each other, let alone coordinate and collaborate in the powerful way that they do. As is, all of these institutions have an interest in the schools successfully performing their core functions and can be contributors to that effort. The founding of the Children's Cabinet (see chapter 3) in Salem (and in other cities supported by EdRedesign Lab efforts, among others) was a policy response in recognition of this fact.

C. J. Huff, the founder and leader of Bright Futures USA, recognized this need for interconnectedness in 2011 when he worked as superintendent in Joplin, Missouri, and a devastating tornado ripped through his community.[22] Indeed, much of the central concept for the Bright Futures model of supporting schools, students, and their families emerged out of that terrible experience. The Bright Futures coordinator in a given school district now serves as a linchpin for accessing needed resources from a broad range of community partners and, perhaps even more critical, helps to develop relationships with those entities that can be activated as needed to address emergencies, big or small.

In Frederick County, this has been exemplified perhaps most singularly in the school district's relationship with the Sheriff's Office. Too often in this country law enforcement agencies are neither seen, nor act, as positive contributors to the well-being of education system stakeholders; as documented above, the performance of sheriff's deputies in their interactions with FCPS officials, students, and their families exemplifies what can happen when these two public entities build a positive connection. From all indications, by doing everything from roller-skating to having lunch with students to collaborating on classroom presentations, deputies have positively influenced the young citizens of Frederick County. This collaboration supports both law enforcement's mission to nurture their relationships with community members as part of their safety responsibilities, and the school district's mission to educate students in a safe and supportive environment. All of this connection inures to the overall benefit of the larger community.

## CONCLUSION

Economic stabilization and community resilience are critical to the success of all communities, but especially to the ISS communities we came to know during the course of our study. While school districts cannot single-handedly control either of these phenomena, failing to recognize the valuable contribution schools can make to community prosperity constitutes a serious error. It also undermines the full extent of public support they deserve and need. If ISS school districts had not assumed a wide array of roles during the pandemic to ensure communities' viability, and had they not continued to act as resource hubs as classrooms returned to a "new normal," it seems likely that, at the very least, ISS communities would be in worse shape than they are today. In fact, there is a strong case to be made that both the ISS schools and the communities they serve are in much better condition than they would have been absent these whole-child, whole-community approaches, and that they may, in the longer term, rebound and rebuild better and stronger.

All the school districts we have discussed are central to the fabric of their localities, in ways that go far beyond the traditional conception of teachers standing in front of classrooms. The economic benefits provided by ISS districts are numerous and, if not always immediately quantifiable, nevertheless real. Beyond the economic stabilization ISS communities can provide during emergency situations, the supports established for students and their families can ultimately lead to enhanced opportunity for individual and family financial success; a reduced need for additional social services and related public expenditures; and local economic growth through the development of a stronger workforce.

# 7

## Lessons Learned: How ISS Approaches Can Alleviate the Impacts of Critical Conditions in Our Nation's Schools

WHILE MUCH HAS BEEN RESEARCHED and written about the importance of integrated student supports (ISS), analysis of its value in the context of the COVID-19 pandemic has, until now, been fairly limited. Although each of the communities studied for the purpose of this book has approached ISS differently and applied and leveraged it in distinct ways over the course of the pandemic and in its aftermath, five cross-cutting lessons emerge from our study that schools and districts across the country can learn from. We hope these lessons will guide education policy and practice going forward.

As discussed, a large share of US schools already operated under emergency circumstances (i.e., in crisis mode) prior to the pandemic, and current conditions suggest that share may well grow in the coming years. So, while these lessons have long been pertinent, acknowledging and embracing them now is urgent. In addition to the ongoing impacts of the pandemic, schools must cope with increasingly frequent societal gun violence, ongoing economic dislocation, and rapidly accelerating climate change, among other things.

The five lessons are not presented in any specific order, and they likely will resonate differently with various educators, policy makers, and community leaders, depending on a district's unique circumstances. But all apply to school systems writ large, and we believe they will reinforce the need to view ISS as a necessary foundation for a broad range of schools, not an "extra" to be adopted within a small subset. Our schools and communities are in "critical condition," and it's past time to adopt more widely a strategy shown not only to be effective in emergencies, but also to enable schools to grow through and beyond them.

## LESSON 1: UNMET NEED IS LIKE AN ICEBERG— THE PART YOU SEE IS JUST THE TIP

For years, if not decades, researchers and advocates have been sounding the alarm about the growing level of unmet needs in the United States— that is, the degree to which households cannot handle their basic needs and are struggling to cope. This manifests at every stage of life, from the uniquely American lack of paid time off to care for new babies to the dire shortage of affordable child care and early learning opportunities, and from widespread retirement insecurity to limited access to caregivers for seniors and those living with disabilities.[1] In reality, the situation is likely more dire than most people know, becoming worse with each economic downturn. What we do know is bad enough. For example, since 2013, over half of all public school students have been eligible for subsidized school meals.[2] In practical terms, this means that, for the past decade, more than one of every two students who step foot inside a public school building lives in a household in which the adults who care for them do not earn enough money to provide for all of that child's basic needs, at least not without making significant compromises to do so.

Partners for Education (PFE, now Partners for Rural Impact) leadership and staff in Appalachian Kentucky describe in stark terms the extreme levels of need they were addressing long before COVID-19 hit. Indeed, Executive Director Dreama Gentry points out that, for communities that have adopted ISS approaches, COVID-19 was not so much a unique crisis as the next in a series that schools were accustomed to tackling. In the decades leading up to the pandemic, the region had suffered from the near-total loss of the coal industry on which it heavily depended; the loss of associated jobs in sectors such as the railroad and small-town businesses; widespread addiction and mass incarceration that left a growing share of children without at least one biological parent; and, most recently, severe floods due to the increasing impacts of climate change. One of the most serious floods took place during the first year of the pandemic, serving to underline the nonstop impact of these crises on the region.

These facts do not take into account the reality that many families are unwilling to acknowledge their need and seek support, or are uncomfortable doing so. Indeed, research on US social services includes studies documenting the stigma associated with accessing help, due in large part to long-standing American narratives and public attitudes that shame people struggling with poverty and exacerbate their related challenges.[3] In schools, this stigma can be seen when applying for subsidized school meals, a complicated, difficult-to-navigate process that sometimes results in students not receiving them.[4] Educators and others we interviewed described many parents' discomfort with applying for subsidized school lunches and their discussions with counselors about the lack of sufficient food in their homes on weekends and over the summer.

Many of our ISS leaders understood this barrier and faced it, head on. In Frederick County, Virginia, for example, former superintendent David Sovine made improving outreach regarding food insecurity and collecting more accurate data on family need one of his SMART goals, so that more families who are eligible for subsidized school meals for their children would apply.[5] In the years preceding the pandemic, Sovine and his team's concern that they did not fully understand the scale and scope of this fundamental gap in information led them to make major progress toward closing it. In turn, this effort gave the district a more realistic sense of the level and scope of community need, and the ability to better support the nutrition of individual members. All of these layers point to the urgency for stronger, more consistent, and more supports-based strategies to identify student, family, and community needs. School communities dedicated to addressing unmet needs should make conducting a needs assessment, a process in which they identify the community's specific needs and available resources, a high priority.

To some extent, the COVID-19 emergency lessened this reluctance to seek assistance. As need became more widespread, accessing services that provided relief naturally lost some of its stigma. As the districts we studied attest, the pandemic seemed to break down certain barriers and spurred more people to ask for help. In Grain Valley, Missouri, a largely middle-class bedroom community, teachers and counselors alike reported a substantial increase in the number of families responding to questions about resources or requesting help. Even in Berea, Kentucky, where need was widespread and apparent long before COVID-19, the educational leaders and ISS program coordinators we spoke with felt that the pandemic had broken down barriers and expanded the share of families who were comfortable asking for, and receiving, support. This trend also points to a strengthening of trust between schools and their communities even beyond where it may have been pre-COVID-19.

Another challenge to assessing accurately the level of need within families is that some may not realize they qualify for, or "deserve," assistance. Just as we have been conditioned to believe, as a society, that asking for help connotes weakness, laziness, or other negative traits, many of us have come to believe that living on the brink is normal.[6] Given these realities, community leaders have long pointed to the challenges of using existing metrics, such as the share of students receiving free or reduced-price meals, and the importance of more robust needs (and asset) assessment.

These barriers to accessing resources speak, too, to the wisdom of supports-based approaches that start from the premise that all students have unmet needs, as well as untapped assets. Built into the ISS strategy is the notion that schools should not wait until students and parents are in a crisis situation, but rather should take action to proactively identify both their needs and assets. In City Connects schools, this means that teachers and coordinators develop personalized plans for each student and tap the student's strengths to ensure no one falls through the cracks because of stigma-based barriers. During the pandemic, in Bright Futures–affiliated districts, such as Frederick County and Grain Valley, this meant that warehouses stocked by community organizations and local and regional businesses with school supplies, clothing, toiletries, and nutritious food could provide for a given student's (and family's) needs in a comprehensive yet diplomatic way. Well-established communication channels among teachers, Bright Futures staff, and community partners helped to identify community members in need. And in North Minneapolis, the Northside Achievement Zone (NAZ)'s family achievement coaches focused their collaboration with parents on helping them cope with increased disruption and serious violence, from getting hot meals delivered on weekends to finding safer, more stable housing.

Taking steps like these reduces or overcomes the barriers that currently prevent too many school and district leaders from understanding the scope and scale of unmet need in their school communities, and thus from effectively alleviating it.

## LESSON 2: SCHOOLS CAN'T GO IT ALONE—THEY NEED PARTNERS

Public schools (and, for that matter, private schools) are not equipped, resourced, or structured to deal with these extensive, and growing, needs. This is particularly true of schools with high-poverty populations, which struggle more acutely and incur both the most immediate and largest funding shortages during economic downturns.[7]

This dynamic is often the first argument presented as to why ISS is not a viable or realistic approach. The same detractors may also note the serious logistical challenges in trying to sort, manage, and coordinate offers of support from potential community partners. But, as the schools highlighted in this book illustrate, those arguments are straw men: schools need not try to "go it alone" nor coordinate dozens of partners. Nor are advocates for community schools and other ISS approaches suggesting they should. While establishing partnerships and administrative flow takes time and effort, a locally responsive ISS structure built into school policy and practice will address many basic needs of a school community and enable schools to run more efficiently and effectively, rather than result in them being overwhelmed.

A diverse set of public and private partners provide a broad range of supports in the school communities we studied. These include the provision of food by the more expected sources—local food pantries and churches—but also by supermarkets and big box stores; as well as less common supports, including the delivery of physical and mental health care by local health-care institutions and community providers. They include both education-related supports, such as tutoring, "lunch buddies," and afterschool programs, and supports with less obvious connection to schooling, such as clothing, housing assistance, furniture, and summer camps.

Schools did not have to coordinate the services provided by all of these various partners on their own, which, traditionally, they are neither structured nor staffed to do. Rather, school districts and ISS organizations funded specific administrative positions (with various names and structures, depending on the model, but often including the term "coordinator") to perform this work. The individuals occupying these positions, such as Nancy Mango in Frederick and Grace McKenzie in Berea, served as collectors and repositories of information about school community needs and assets. They also served as organizers and relationship managers for the many community partners and their various services.

In Salem, Massachusetts, the assistant principal of Collins Middle School, Michael Titus, shared his appreciation for City Connects coordinators Mia Riccio and Brad Maloon:

> They have this sort of interface with our families that I don't get to have just by the nature of my role. I try to be a very supportive administrator . . . but at the end of the day a lot of my conversations are going to be when your kid made a mistake. And now we need to have that discipline conversation. . . . I'm never going to be able to do it the same way as Brad and Mia, which is, "Hey! We've got a full turkey dinner that we want you to be able to come pick up so you can have a Thanksgiving meal." And that's necessary. I can't be both those people. It would blur lines too much.[8]

These ISS coordinators serve as the link—a connection point—among schools, their communities, and service-providing partner organizations. And, as the pandemic demonstrated, this circulatory system works well. Both existing and potential partners understood this structure and stepped forward to expand existing services and/or volunteer new ones as needs changed and grew over subsequent years. Our ISS communities demonstrated that when a transparent network of local support has been established, current and new partners are able to lend their support quickly and efficiently, even amidst a crisis.

These examples also illuminate another important reality: partners do not just provide benefits to schools; they also benefit from these relationships. YMCAs and Boys & Girls Clubs that can use space, rent-free, in a school, and that do not have to work to recruit participants or transport them to their own spaces, can operate more efficiently and at lower cost. Health-care providers with access to information about physical and mental health needs among students and families can better target their limited resources where they are needed most and, again, often at lower cost.

Moreover, prevention is exponentially more cost-effective and less expensive than remediation or, all too often when prevention is lacking, crisis response. And, as Ascension Catholic School principal Benito Matias emphasizes, absent NAZ's role as community "glue," many of these North Minneapolis partners would never have the chance to meet one another, let alone sit at the same table to shape policies and practices that ensure more students are school-ready and become college- and career-ready.[9]

## LESSON 3: THERE IS NO COOKIE-CUTTER APPROACH TO ISS

Every community has its own set of needs and assets, and those evolve over time. Even successful models that have been replicated dozens of times, such as those of Bright Futures and City Connects (or Full-Service Community Schools [FSCS], which describe themselves as strategies, not models) can look somewhat different when applied in different school communities. The ISS districts we studied have been effective because they have developed a deep understanding of the communities in which they are located and, drawing on both their own resources and those of their partners, have devised solutions that meet the moment and the place. Certainly, at the onset of COVID-19, ISS communities demonstrated their ability to build upon previous successful efforts and to pivot to new approaches that were needed to address identified needs. While many of the same issues and similar solutions could be found in these communities, there were important differences.

Because the communities we studied employed a variety of models and strategies—Bright Futures, City Connects, FSCS, Promise Neighborhoods—they appropriately look different in their implementation. In Frederick County, the Sheriff's Office stepped up to deliver meals and check in on families, while in Salem, school staff and City Connects coordinators reached out via phone to every family, working with a range of partners to meet needs and fill gaps those calls identified. In North Minneapolis, NAZ's family achievement coaches made sure all the families on their list were aware of and had access to any ISS services they needed. In both Eastern Appalachia and Grain Valley, ISS leadership teams recognized the need to increase socio-emotional support for students, teachers, and families. Their leading ISS agents, PFE and Bright Futures, respectively, jumped into action in various ways, such as by increasing the number of counselors and social workers, integrating new activities like yoga, and creating new spaces within the schools to support mental health and well-being.

As these communities demonstrated, the ISS approach is not a static, cookie-cutter model that can be picked up and applied straight out of the box. While a quick and uniform solution may, on the surface, appear easier, as proponents of other education reform efforts have argued, these approaches often do not meet the diversity of community needs, fail to tap extensive (but overlooked) community assets, and cannot be sustained long term. The dynamic nature of the ISS approach and its emphasis on context and meaningful relationships propels its success beyond many previous efforts. The ISS approach allows for the school's support services network to adapt and change as the community changes or experiences new emergencies, like the COVID-19 pandemic. Each of these ISS communities' similar yet distinct applications of this approach should be seen as a strength, and as necessary for promoting community resilience and prosperity.

## LESSON 4: TEACHERS AND SCHOOL STAFF NEED TO RECEIVE SOCIAL-EMOTIONAL SUPPORT, TOO

Being on the front lines of tackling poverty is exhausting and mentally and emotionally taxing. The COVID-19 emergency made this long-standing reality even more true, and even more visible. When the pandemic hit, these traumas were both illuminated and sharply elevated.

In the ISS communities we studied, teachers carried huge burdens. The student and family needs they had been trained to identify and address rose rapidly, and while the webs of community partnerships that had been put in place were deployed to great effect, unmet needs still continued to rise. These districts were much better prepared than most to shift to remote learning and to quickly ensure that all, or the vast majority, of students had the devices they needed to access virtual classrooms and the internet connections to support that access.

Nonetheless, engagement was a struggle, especially in households challenged by poverty, rising stress, the threat of eviction, and parents working essential jobs, with people facing daily the threat of exposure to COVID-19, illness, hospitalization, and even death, especially in the year before the vaccine was widely available.

All of these challenges and the intense emotions that came with them made their way into virtual classrooms, with teachers often being the first adults outside of the family to bear witness to how a student was coping with these many stressors. Teachers and school leaders such as Nathan Perry in Grain Valley, Michael Titus in Salem, Athena Deaton in Berea, and Suzanne Miller in Frederick shared stories about how the pandemic brought these struggles to the forefront and the added lengths they and their colleagues went to in supporting their students.

Adding to the burden, Deaton pointed to the shortage of available substitute teachers, especially during the height of the pandemic, which added pressure to teachers to stay on the job, even when physically ill or in need of a mental health day—although, both Deaton and Perry noted, their administrations were supportive of teachers' need for rest and time for self-care.[10] Focused, healthy teachers are the bedrock of a school community and, as such, are critical foundations of the ISS strategy. Prior to the COVID-19 crisis, the degree to which teachers experienced secondary trauma, especially those in schools with high concentrations of poverty, had not received the attention it deserved. The stories teachers shared in the ISS communities we studied highlight the importance of acknowledging and addressing secondary traumas so educators can be their best selves, both for their own health and for the students who need them.

On the other side of the equation, active student engagement became more and more sparse during the pandemic. While, in theory, students and teachers were interacting in virtual settings, in reality there was often little authentic interaction between the two groups, depriving both of the nurturing that face-to-face instruction provides. Teachers who spent their days "talking" to a mostly black screen describe the confusion, frustration, and concern they felt on behalf of students who might be trying to learn in contexts that made them reluctant to show their faces or bedrooms. Many of our educators said these experiences contributed to increased burnout among their colleagues, leading to early retirement or career changes, mirroring national trends.[11]

Perhaps most concerning, teachers feared for their physical safety and watched fellow educators die as they did their essential jobs. As noted in chapter 3, in Appalachian Kentucky, one small county lost two school staff, including a teacher, in a single month early in the pandemic.[12] Given they did not yet have the protection afforded by vaccines, and did not know when that protection would be available, these events created tremendous stress among educators. Grace McKenzie, associate director of family partnerships with PFE, observed how such losses created a ripple effect through the school community as she tried to manage decisions of modality and safety: "Parents are trying to help their children navigate the loss of people who cared for them at the school and the school is trying to navigate the mental health and support for that. At the same time, schools and families are trying to navigate the continual back and forth of 'Are we in school, or are we not in school?'"[13]

The reality of schools being and becoming a life-threatening work environment was evident in the multiple communities that we studied. In NAZ, students have been living and teachers have been working in literal war zones. This deeply segregated and economically and socially isolated section of Minneapolis was dubbed "Murderopolis" in the mid-1990s for its historically high level of violent crime.[14] More recently, the area has become known as "Ground Zero" for civil unrest and ongoing violence since the May 25, 2020 murder of George Floyd spurred nationwide protests and calls for police reform.[15] Teachers are living in the midst of what NAZ cofounder and CEO Sondra Samuels describes as "unrelenting violence"—trying to teach students who are witnessing that violence, including the murder of family and friends, while fearing for their own lives and mourning their students and other children who are being killed in the community.[16]

NAZ family achievement coach Tatika Taylor lost her own uncle to police gun violence when she was a girl, the day before her twelfth birthday. She is far from alone in revisiting personal tragedy as she helps the next generation of youth in North Minneapolis cope with their own experiences of violence, and even murder, at the hands of police. She also speaks for many other educators and mentors in emphasizing the need to address such traumas proactively. Having not received such support herself, she doubles down on the importance of ensuring that today's NAZ scholars receive it.[17]

The literature is replete with stories of the hardships suffered by the US teacher workforce during the pandemic and how those experiences have impacted workers since. The educators we spoke with in ISS communities certainly faced as many difficulties as anyone, and freely acknowledged their personal challenges. Our sense, though, is that because of the collaborative leadership and resource-rich models in place, educators in ISS schools fared better than most of their peers in non-ISS districts. Indeed, given the serious struggles and traumas they encountered, it is hard to imagine what the experience of this emergency was like for teachers in non-ISS communities that lacked strong, multifaceted support from school and district leadership and their communities more broadly. Several of the people we interviewed said as much, expressing deep gratitude for the added resources.

Taking these lessons to heart, we contend that beginning with preservice training and continuing with ongoing professional development, teachers in schools across the country would benefit from more and better education regarding tools for coping with the various workplace-related traumas that are part of this important work. We recommend that ISS communities and others alike invest in strategies and support systems for their educators' social-emotional well-being as well as access to school partners who can supplement their own work with specific expertise for handling all that now confronts our teachers on a daily basis.

## LESSON 5: WHILE ISS IS A CRITICALLY IMPORTANT TREATMENT LEADING TO BETTER OUTCOMES, IT IS NOT THE SOLUTION TO THESE ONGOING EMERGENCIES

Sondra Samuels articulated this reality most clearly. In April 2023, when many were describing the context in which schools were operating as "post-pandemic," Samuels reflected on the ironic duality her community faced. NAZ had grown enormously over the decade-plus since its founding in 2010 and its first Promise Neighborhoods grant in 2011. At its inception, NAZ's operating budget was $450,000, which supported a staff of three, complemented by AmeriCorps volunteers. It now employs sixty staff, with a senior membership team of five and an annual budget of $14 million. The robust early childhood program NAZ had established was expanding to include doula services and prenatal home visits for pregnant women, and at the time of the interview, Samuels was in the process of signing papers for the new operations facility the organization had recently purchased.[18]

All these benchmarks of progress proved that NAZ's comprehensive, wraparound, family-centered approach was driving progress among its "scholars." Yet, as Samuels notes, with those scholars—children—reeling and working to recover from the dual crisis of the pandemic and the murder of George Floyd, along with the ongoing, unrelenting violence that has spiked in the years since, they have lost much, perhaps most, of the academic ground they gained in prior years. Indeed, the reason for the new building was the inability of Samuels's leadership staff and educators to safely meet and work in their old space, where mental bandwidth was split between helping students and monitoring the violence outside.[19] And Samuels recounts losing children on a regular basis— some were shot by fellow students, others murdered by police, and a middle school student was killed when the car he and a fellow student had stolen crashed into a pole, crushing him. Children and their families are living with constant trauma, as are their teachers.

Notwithstanding the heroic work being done across Appalachian Kentucky, a large and growing share of children in that region are also living with severe, ongoing trauma. The widespread trend in joblessness that has little prospect of turning around drives despair that often translates into alcohol and drug abuse, addiction, and incarceration or even death. Aunts, uncles, grandparents, and neighbors try to pick up the slack, and schools supported by Partners for Rural Impact provide a range of supports to help with that effort. But too many children are growing up with emotional scars that will be difficult to heal, and teachers bemoan the reality that, for the majority, there is little hope of improving their circumstances while continuing to live in their local communities. Educators are forced to encourage their students to leave—to take internships, go to college, and ultimately find jobs and build adult lives and careers elsewhere, leaving their hometowns even less likely to recover.

Even in largely middle-class Grain Valley, Missouri, and in other less impoverished communities we have studied over the years, lack of affordable housing and homelessness have reached crisis proportions. In those cities and in Frederick County, educators report record-high and rising levels of student anxiety and mental health problems among ever-younger children that they struggle to wrap their heads around, let alone address. And as emphasized in chapter 1, when gun violence strikes a community, its effects ripple far beyond a school's walls, a neighborhood's roads, and even an entire community's borders. So, while ISS strategies work hard to contend with these realities, and are needed and effective to a large degree, they cannot prevent or erase the harsh impacts of these widespread crises.

The pandemic, and its ongoing impacts, brought this reality to the national consciousness. As Ascension Catholic School principal Benito Matias rightly notes:

> It's going to take time, I think, for us to really realize, understand, absorb, process the full impact [of COVID-19]. Because it has touched every single corner of every single person's life on this planet, and in our lifetime, we've just never experienced that. And so the patience, the empathy, the compassion, has been greatly diminished. Not just amongst adults, but I see that with kids. There's a heightened anxiety among them. . . . We have families in which the primary caretaker lost their job, or they lost their home, or their lifestyle changed dramatically, because someone in the family got sick or passed away from COVID. I mean, clearly, lives changed forever.[20]

Having the myriad NAZ partners to turn to, lean on, and collaborate with has literally been a game-changer and lifesaver for Matias and his colleagues. And he says that, until we have these conversations across the country and make such supports-based networks the norm, rather than the exception, the vast majority of other students whose daily lives are similar to those of his scholars and their families will fall off the cliffs that we, as a society, have put them on.

PRI's Dreama Gentry, who has been doing this work for over thirty-five years, echoes this sentiment. The COVID-19 pandemic, she believes, brought home to wealthier districts across the country stark realities with which her remote Appalachian region, North Minneapolis, and many other, similarly less visible communities have struggled for decades.

My husband's African American, so our kids are African American, and I think George Floyd being murdered was horrendous, and it opened a lot of eyes, but . . . one of the things [my husband] said is, "You know, nothing changed from yesterday. It was just, you know, it was always like this, right?" We always had to deal with it. And so I think that . . . what I'm hoping is that the system of education and supporting children and families, COVID will open their eyes to the reality that every school should have this safety net and support net that community schools can provide. They should just be in place.[21]

As a nation, we have de facto come to unreasonably expect our schools to be "the answer" for a depressingly long list of social challenges. The COVID-19 pandemic highlighted for many just how important a role our educators and schools play in, essentially, holding our communities together. Yet, we do not provide them with the support they need to do this daunting work. Even districts that have recognized the value of providing ISS are "swimming upstream" against a litany of crises—poverty, gun violence, culture wars, homelessness, impacts of climate change ranging from excessive heat to natural disasters—and they know, and we must recognize, that even FSCS is not a panacea for the structural inequalities that have come to characterize American society.

Most of our schools cannot successfully fulfill their educational mission unless our country is serious about tackling those crises mentioned above, as well as other important issues. Our research has convinced us, and we hope this book has convinced you, that we need more schools offering ISS, for all of the good they can do. In their communities, ISS schools play an essential role in helping to address ongoing and sudden crises. And, as we have also argued, they make communities much better prepared for the next ones. No matter how impressive their performance, though, we should all agree, too, that doing all we can to eliminate the crises altogether is a better strategy than letting them continue to take their massive toll, while asking our schools and our education professionals to minimize the impacts.

While the challenges and crises described in this book have, for too long, been framed as education problems and relegated to schools to solve, the reality that they are much larger and have broad societal impacts demands similarly larger political action at the local, state, and national levels. We are encouraged to see rapidly growing momentum around community schools and whole-child, supports-based approaches more broadly. We hope that readers will work to expand that momentum and call on their leaders to take robust action, so that communities, students, families, and schools across the country finally receive the full range of supports they need to thrive.

# NOTES

## INTRODUCTION

1. For more on "education in emergencies," see UNESCO, "Why Does UNESCO Consider Education So Important in Times of Emergency?," last modified June 15, 2023, https://www.unesco.org/en/emergencies/education/need-know#:~:text =UNESCO%20considers%20education%20an%20immediate,hampered%20 in%20times%20of%20emergency.

2. Save the Children, *Attacks on Education: The Impact of Conflict and Grave Violations on Children's Future*, 2013, https://www.savethechildren.org/content/dam /global/reports/education-and-child-protection/attacks-on-ed-2013.pdf.

3. Nyasha Tirivayi et al., "A Rapid Review of Economic Policy and Social Protection Responses with Health and Economic Crises and Their Effects on Children: Lessons for the COVID-19 Pandemic Response," UNICEF Office of Research, Innocenti Working Paper 2020-02, June 2020, https://www.unicef-irc .org/publications/1095-rapid-review-economic-policy-social-protection -responses-to-health-and-economic-crises.html.

4. Centers for Disease Control and Prevention, "CDC Museum COVID-19 Timeline," accessed March 15, 2023, https://www.cdc.gov/museum/timeline/covid19.html.

5. Frances C. Fowler, *Policy Studies for Educational Leaders: An Introduction*, 4th ed. (Boston: Pearson Education, 2013).

6. Katie Reilly, "Some Parents Are Demanding In-Person Schooling as the Pandemic Stretches On," *Time*, October 23, 2020, https://time.com/5903082/parents -coronavirus-schools/.

7. Linda Darling-Hammond, Abby Schachner, and Adam K. Edgerton, *Restarting and Reinventing School: Learning in the Time of COVID and Beyond*, Learning Policy Institute, August 2020, https://files.eric.ed.gov/fulltext/ED610890.pdf.

8. Emma García and Elaine Weiss, *COVID-19 and Student Performance, Equity, and US Education Policy: Lessons from Pre-Pandemic Research to Inform Relief,*

*Recovery, and Rebuilding,* Economic Policy Institute, September 10, 2020, https://files.eric.ed.gov/fulltext/ED610971.pdf.

9. García and Weiss, *COVID-19 and Student Performance.*

10. Kristin Seefeldt, John D. Graham, and Gordon Abner, *America's Poor and the Great Recession* (Bloomington: Indiana University Press, 2013).

11. Steve Suitts, "The Worst of Times: Children in Extreme Poverty in the South and Nation," *Southern Spaces,* June 29, 2010, https://southernspaces.org/2010/worst-times-children-extreme-poverty-south-and-nation/#:~:text=At%20least%20two%20out%20of,of%20extreme%20poverty%20among%20children.

12. William J. Mathis and Tina M. Trujillo, eds., *Learning from the Federal Market-Based Reforms: Lessons for ESSA* (Charlotte, NC: Information Age Publishing, 2016), 95.

13. Mathis and Trujillo, *Learning,* 95.

14. William J. Mathis and Tina M. Trujillo, "School Reform: What Went Wrong, What Went Right, and What We Should Do in the Future," *Washington Post,* September 19, 2016, https://www.washingtonpost.com/news/answer-sheet/wp/2016/09/19/school-reform-what-went-wrong-what-went-right-and-what-we-should-do-in-the-future/.

15. Hal A. Lawson and Dolf Van Veen, eds., *Developing Community Schools, Community Learning Centers, Extended-Service Schools and Multi-Service Schools: International Exemplars for Practice, Policy and Research* (New York: Springer, 2015).

16. Jennifer Jellison Holme et al., "Community Schools as an Urban School Reform Strategy: Examining Partnerships, Governance, and Sustainability Through the Lens of the Full-Service Community Schools Grant Program," *Educational Policy* 36, no. 3 (2022): 520–549.

17. See Elaine Weiss and Paul Reville, *Broader, Bolder, Better: How Schools and Communities Help Students Overcome the Disadvantages of Poverty* (Cambridge, MA: Harvard University Press, 2019); and Paul Reville and Lynne Sacks, *Collaborative Action for Equity and Opportunity: A Practical Guide for School and Community Leaders* (Cambridge, MA: Harvard University Press, 2021).

## CHAPTER 1

1. *Merriam-Webster* Dictionary, s.v. "Emergency," accessed February 27, 2024, https://www.merriam-webster.com/dictionary/emergency.

2. OECD, "CO2.2 Child Poverty," OECD Family Database, August 2021, https://www.oecd.org/els/CO_2_2_Child_Poverty.pdf.

3. Lyndon B. Johnson, "Annual Message to the Congress on the State of the Union," The American Presidency Project, January 08, 1964, https://www.presidency.ucsb.edu/documents/annual-message-the-congress-the-state-the-union-25.

4. Robert A. Moffitt, "The Great Recession and the Social Safety Net," *Annals of the American Academy of Political and Social Science* 650, no. 1 (2013): 143–166.

5. Ajay Chaudry et al., *Poverty in the United States: 50-Year Trends and Safety Net Impacts*, US Department of Health and Human Services, March 2016, https://aspe.hhs.gov/sites/default/files/migrated_legacy_files//142581/50Year Trends.pdf.

6. Chaudry et al., *Poverty in the United States*.

7. Chaudry et al., *Poverty in the United States*.

8. Suzanne Macartney and Robin Ghertner, *How Many People That Receive One Safety Net Benefit Also Receive Others?*, US Department of Health and Human Services, January 2023, https://aspe.hhs.gov/sites/default/files/documents/34 0f9d2586febc3cdc1510f793403d0c/program-overlap-datapoint.pdf.

9. Rebecca M. Blank and Maria J. Hanratty, "Responding to Need: A Comparison of Social Safety Nets in Canada and the United States," in *Small Differences That Matter: Labor Markets and Income Maintenance in Canada and the United States*, ed. David Card and Richard B. Freeman (Chicago: University of Chicago Press, 1993), 191–232.

10. Barry Bluestone, *The Deindustrialization of America: Plant Closings, Community Abandonment, and the Dismantling of Basic Industry* (New York: Basic Books, 1984).

11. William Serrin, "Collapse of Our Industrial Heartland," *New York Times Magazine*, June 6, 1982, https://www.nytimes.com/1982/06/06/magazine/collapse -of-our-industrial-heartland.html.

12. Daniel Hartley, "Urban Decline in Rust-Belt Cities," Federal Reserve Bank of Cleveland Economic Commentary No. 2013-06, May 20, 2013.

13. Steven High, *Industrial Sunset: The Making of North America's Rustbelt, 1969–1984* (Toronto: University of Toronto Press, 2003), 15.

14. Kathryn Marie Dudley, *The End of the Line: Lost Jobs, New Lives in Postindustrial America* (Chicago: University of Chicago Press, 1994).

15. Dana L. Mitra, Marcela Movit, and William Frick, "Brain Drain in the Rust Belt: Can Educational Reform Help to Build Civic Capacity in Struggling Communities?," *Educational Policy* 22, no. 5 (2008): 731–757.

16. Others, like Binghamton, New York, which experienced a more recent population exodus, have repositioned themselves as college towns. As a 2020 dissertation exploring factors preventing nontraditional college students from completing their degrees illustrates, the cultural divides that result can create a culture clash for children raised by noncollege educated families; Thomas R. Quain, "Leaving College Without a Degree: Oral Histories from the Rust-Belt" (PhD diss., State University of New York at Binghamton, 2020).

17. Sean Safford, *Why the Garden Club Couldn't Save Youngstown: The Transformation of the Rust Belt* (Cambridge, MA: Harvard University Press, 2009).

18. Kathryn A. Edwards, "Recovered, but Not Whole: U.S. Jobs Rebounded, but Not for Everyone," *The RAND Blog*, July 18, 2022, https://www.rand.org/blog /2022/07/recovered-but-not-whole-us-jobs-rebounded.html.

19. Georgetown University Center on Education and the Workforce, "Tracking COVID-19 Unemployment and Job Losses," 2020, https://cew.georgetown.edu /cew-reports/jobtracker/.

20. Christy Mach Dube and Elizabeth Brodbine Ghoniem, *Ending Hunger in Our Classrooms: Expanding After-the-Bell Breakfast to Fuel Student Learning*, Second Annual Massachusetts School Breakfast Report Card, Eos Foundation, 2018, https://www.riseandshinema.org/wp-content/uploads/2018/05/MA-School -Breakfast-Report-Card-2018.pdf.

21. Alisha Coleman-Jensen et al., "Household Food Security in the United States in 2019," US Department of Agriculture, September 2020, https://www.ers.usda .gov/webdocs/publications/104656/err-309.pdf.

22. Lauren Bauer, "About 14 Million Children in the U.S. Are Not Getting Enough to Eat," Brookings Institution, July 9, 2020, https://www.brookings.edu/articles /about-14-million-children-in-the-us-are-not-getting-enough-to-eat/.

23. Bauer, "About 14 Million Children."

24. US Department of Agriculture, "National School Lunch Program," https://www .fns.usda.gov/nslp.

25. Andrew Aurand, *The Gap: A Shortage of Affordable Homes*, National Low Income Housing Coalition, 2020, https://reports.nlihc.org/sites/default/files /gap/Gap-Report_2020.pdf; Stacy Sirmans and David Macpherson, "The State of Affordable Housing," *Journal of Real Estate Literature* 11, no. 2 (2003): 131–156.

26. Richard Rothstein, *The Color of Law: A Forgotten History of How Our Government Segregated America* (New York: Liveright Publishing, 2017).

27. Keeanga-Yamahtta Taylor, *Race for Profit: How Banks and the Real Estate Industry Undermined Black Homeownership* (Chapel Hill: University of North Carolina Press, 2019).

28. Mehrsa Baradaran, *The Color of Money: Black Banks and the Racial Wealth Gap* (Cambridge, MA: Harvard University Press, 2017).

29. Christopher Cleveland and Dylan Lukes, "The Lingering Legacy of Redlining on School Funding, Diversity, and Performance," EdWorkingPaper No. 21-363, Annenberg Institute for School Reform at Brown University, 2022, https://files .eric.ed.gov/fulltext/ED616673.pdf.

30. Michael C. Lens, "Extremely Low-Income Households, Housing Affordability and the Great Recession," *Urban Studies* 55, no. 8 (2018): 1615–1635; Aurand, "The Gap."

31. Anastasia Kalugina, "Affordable Housing Policies: An Overview," Cornell Baker Program in Real Estate, 2016, https://ecommons.cornell.edu/bitstream /handle/1813/70761/Affordable_Housing_Overview.pdf.

32. Kristin Seefeldt, John D. Graham, and Gordon Abner, *America's Poor and the Great Recession* (Bloomington: Indiana University Press, 2013).

33. Kalugina, "Affordable Housing Policies."
34. Matthew Desmond, *Evicted: Poverty and Profit in the American City* (New York: Crown/Archetype, 2016).
35. Lens, "Extremely Low-Income Households," 1618.
36. Katherine Schaeffer, "Key Facts About Housing Affordability in the U.S.," Pew Research Center, March 23, 2022, https://www.pewresearch.org/fact-tank/2022/03/23/key-facts-about-housing-affordability-in-the-u-s/.
37. Federal Reserve Bank of New York, "Inflation Expectations Decline Across All Horizons," press release, August 8, 2022, https://www.newyorkfed.org/newsevents/news/research/2022/20220808.
38. Jerusalem Demsas, "Covid-19 Caused a Recession. So Why Did the Housing Market Boom?," *Vox*, February 5, 2021, https://www.vox.com/22264268/covid-19-housing-insecurity-housing-prices-mortgage-rates-pandemic-zoning-supply-demand.
39. Maria Massimo, "Housing as a Right in the United States: Mitigating the Affordable Housing Crisis Using an International Human Rights Law Approach," *Boston College Law Review* 62 (2021): 273–314.
40. Sheila Crowley, "The Affordable Housing Crisis: Residential Mobility of Poor Families and School Mobility of Poor Children," *Journal of Negro Education* 72, no. 1 (2003): 22–38; Elizabeth J. Mueller and J. Rosie Tighe, "Making the Case for Affordable Housing: Connecting Housing with Health and Education Outcomes," *Journal of Planning Literature* 21, no. 4 (2007): 371–385.
41. Abraham Maslow and K. J. Lewis, "Maslow's Hierarchy of Needs," *Salenger Incorporated* 14, no. 17 (1987): 987–990.
42. Meghan Henry et al., *The 2021 Annual Homeless Assessment Report (AHAR) to Congress*, US Department of Housing and Urban Development, Office of Community Planning and Development, February 2022, https://www.huduser.gov/portal/sites/default/files/pdf/2021-AHAR-Part-1.pdf.
43. Henry et al., "2020 Annual Homeless Assessment."
44. Lisa A. Goodman, Leonard Saxe, and Mary Harvey, "Homelessness as Psychological Trauma: Broadening Perspectives," *American Psychologist* 46, no. 11 (1991): 1219–1225.
45. See https://www.hud.gov/press/press_releases_media_advisories/hud_no_23_278.
46. Alexandra E. Pavlakis and Barbara Duffield, "The Politics of Policy in the McKinney–Vento Homeless Assistance Act: Setting the Agenda for Students Experiencing Homelessness," *Urban Review* 49 (2017): 805–831.
47. National Center for Education Statistics, *State Nonfiscal Public Elementary/Secondary Education Survey Data*, Common Core of Data, accessed September 13, 2021, https://nces.ed.gov/ccd/stnfis.asp, school years 2017–2018 (v.1a), 2018–2019 (v.1a), and 2019–2020 (v.1a).

48. Soledad De Gregorio et al., "Timing and Duration of Student Homelessness and Educational Outcomes in Los Angeles," *Educational Researcher* 51, no. 6 (2022): 376–386.

49. Jelena Obradović et al., "Academic Achievement of Homeless and Highly Mobile Children in an Urban School District: Longitudinal Evidence on Risk, Growth, and Resilience," *Development and Psychopathology* 21, no. 2 (2009): 493–518; Angie C. Kennedy, "Homelessness, Violence Exposure, and School Participation Among Urban Adolescent Mothers," *Journal of Community Psychology* 35, no. 5 (2007): 639–654.

50. Peter M. Miller, "A Critical Analysis of the Research on Student Homelessness," *Review of Educational Research* 81, no. 3 (2011): 308–337.

51. De Gregorio et al., "Timing and Duration."

52. Lynnette Mawhinney-Rhoads and Gerald Stahler, "Educational Policy and Reform for Homeless Students: An Overview," *Education and Urban Society* 38, no. 3 (2006): 288–306.

53. Alex M. Wagaman et al., "The Role of Schools in Supporting Students Experiencing Homelessness: Perceptions of School Staff," *Children & Schools* 44, no. 2 (2022): 70–78.

54. Stacey A. Havlik et al., "'Do Whatever You Can to Try to Support That Kid': School Counselors' Experiences Addressing Student Homelessness," *Professional School Counseling* 21, no. 1 (2017): 47–59.

55. Peter M. Miller, "A Critical Analysis of the Research on Student Homelessness," *Review of Educational Research* 81, no. 3 (2011): 308–337.

56. Miller, "Critical Analysis"; Wagaman et al., "Role of Schools."

57. Richard Nixon Foundation, "Public Enemy Number One: A Pragmatic Approach to America's Drug Problem," June 29, 2016, https://www.nixonfoundation.org/2016/06/26404/.

58. Kenneth B. Nunn, "Race, Crime and the Pool of Surplus Criminality: Or Why the 'War on Drugs' Was a 'War on Blacks,'" *Journal of Gender Race & Justice* 6 (2002): 381.

59. Nunn, "Race, Crime and the Pool," 381.

60. Nkechi Taifa et al., "Race, Mass Incarceration, and the Disastrous War on Drugs: Unravelling Decades of Racially Biased Anti-Drug Policies Is a Monumental Project," Brennan Center for Justice, May 10, 2021, https://www.brennancenter.org/our-work/analysis-opinion/race-mass-incarceration-and-disastrous-war-drugs.

61. Michelle Alexander, *The New Jim Crow: Mass Incarceration in the Age of Colorblindness* (New York: New Press, 2012).

62. Alexia Cooper and Erica L. Smith, *Homicide Trends in the United States, 1980–2008* (Washington, DC: Bureau of Justice Statistics, 2011).

63. Alexander, *New Jim Crow*, 7.

64. Alexander, *New Jim Crow*, 8.

65. Dorothy E. Roberts, "The Social Moral Cost of Mass Incarceration in African American Communities," *Stanford Law Review* 56 (2003): 1271–1305.

66. Nazgol Ghandnoosh, "Voting Rights in the Era of Mass Incarceration: A Primer," The Sentencing Project, July 28, 2021, https://www.sentencingproject .org/policy-brief/voting-rights-in-the-era-of-mass-incarceration-a-primer/.

67. William Julius Wilson and Kathryn M. Neckerman, "Poverty and Family Structure: The Widening Gap Between Evidence and Public Policy Issues," in *Fighting Poverty: What Works and What Doesn't*, ed. S. H. Danziger and D. H. Weinberg (Cambridge, MA: Harvard University Press, 1987), 232–259.

68. Anne Case and Angus Deaton, *Deaths of Despair and the Future of Capitalism* (Princeton, NJ: Princeton University Press, 2020).

69. Leadership Conference for Civil Rights Education Fund, "The 'War on Drugs' Has Failed, Commission Says," June 2011, https://civilrights.org/edfund/resource/the -war-on-drugs-has-failed-commission-says/.

70. Christopher J. Coyne and Abigail Hall, "Four Decades and Counting: The Continued Failure of the War on Drugs," Policy Analysis No. 811, Cato Institute, April 12, 2017, https://www.cato.org/policy-analysis/four-decades-counting -continued-failure-war-drugs.

71. Federal Bureau of Investigation, *Crime in the United States, 2013* (Washington, DC: Department of Justice, 2014).

72. Peter Reuter, "Why Has US Drug Policy Changed So Little over 30 Years?," *Crime and Justice* 42, no. 1 (2013): 75–140.

73. For example, "One study of Virginia found that cities, towns, and counties with the highest percentages of Black residents and low-income residents charge higher fines and fees compared to the state average. Another report, written in 2008 for the Washington State Minority and Justice Commission, found courts assessed higher fines or fees on Latinx people than on their white counterparts. The disproportionate impacts of fines and fees cement historical and generational wealth disparities for communities of color." Cortney Sanders and Michael Leachman, "Step One to an Antiracist State Revenue Policy: Eliminate Criminal Justice Fees and Reform Fines," Center on Budget and Policy Priorities, September 17, 2021, https://www.cbpp.org/research/state-budget-and-tax /step-one-to-an-antiracist-state-revenue-policy-eliminate-criminal.

74. Linda Plitt Donaldson and Diane Yentel, "The Drug War, Mass Incarceration and Race," Drug Policy Alliance, June 2015, https://www.unodc.org/documents /ungass2016/Contributions/Civil/DrugPolicyAlliance/DPA_Fact_Sheet_Drug _War_Mass_Incarceration_and_Race_June2015.pdf.

75. Christopher J. Mumola, *Incarcerated Parents and Their Children*, Bureau of Justice Statistics Special Report, Department of Justice Office of Justice Programs, August 2000, https://bjs.ojp.gov/content/pub/pdf/iptc.pdf.

76. Leila Morsy and Richard Rothstein, *Mass Incarceration and Children's Outcomes: Criminal Justice Policy Is Education Policy*, Education Policy Institute,

December 2016, https://www.epi.org/publication/mass-incarceration-and -childrens-outcomes/.

77. Macartney and Ghertner, *How Many People?*, 1.

78. NASA, "What Is Climate Change?," accessed February 27, 2024, https://climate .nasa.gov/what-is-climate-change/.

79. Christine Hauser and Claire Moses, "Smoke Pollution from Canadian Wildfires Blankets U.S. Cities, Again," *New York Times*, July 17, 2023, https://www.nytimes .com/2023/07/17/us/wildfire-smoke-canada-ny-air-quality.html.

80. Brady Dennis and Joyce Koh, "Smoke from Canadian Wildfires Engulfs East Coast, Upending Daily Life," *Washington Post*, June 7, 2023, https://www .washingtonpost.com/climate-environment/2023/06/07/air-quality-nyc-us -canada-wildfire-smoke/.

81. Solcyre Burga, "Why the Maui Wildfires Were So Deadly," *Time*, August 15, 2023, https://time.com/6305113/maui-wildfire-cause-hawaii/#.

82. Katie Worth, "Kids Are Living with Climate Catastrophe. That Doesn't Mean They Believe in It," *Washington Post*, November 10, 2021, https://www.washingtonpost .com/outlook/2021/11/10/climate-change-education-students/.

83. Katie Reckdahl, "The Lost Children of Katrina," *Atlantic*, April 2, 2015, https:// www.theatlantic.com/education/archive/2015/04/the-lost-children-of-katrina /389345/.

84. Alexa Lardieri, "Another Victim of the California Wildfires: Education," *U.S. News & World Report*, October 31, 2019, https://www.usnews.com/news /education-news/articles/2019-10-31/another-victim-of-the-california-wildfires -education.

85. Erin Digitale, "How to Climate-Proof Schools: Revamping Schools to With-stand What's Coming," Stanford Medicine, June 2, 2023, https://stanmed .stanford.edu/climate-resiliency-schools/.

86. Emily Cochrane, "'We'll Teach Out of Anywhere': In Flooded Kentucky, Schools Race to Rebuild," *New York Times*, August 28, 2022, https://www.nytimes.com /2022/08/28/us/kentucky-flooding-schools.html.

87. Arianna Prothero, "Nearly Half of Educators Say Climate Change Is Affect-ing Their Schools—or Will Soon," *Education Week*, May 23, 2022, https://www .edweek.org/leadership/nearly-half-of-educators-say-climate-change-is -affecting-their-schools-or-will-soon/2022/05.

88. Caroline Hickman et al., "Climate Anxiety in Children and Young People and Their Beliefs About Government Responses to Climate Change: A Global Sur-vey," *Lancet Planetary Health* 5, no. 12 (2021): e863–e873.

89. Laura Meckler, "The Heat Wave Is Shutting Schools Down Just as Kids Return to Class," *Washington Post*, September 6, 2023, https://www.washingtonpost .com/education/2023/09/06/schools-heat-wave-closures-early-dismissals/.

90. National Oceanic and Atmospheric Administration, "The World Just Sweltered Through Its Hottest August on Record," September 14, 2023, https://www.noaa

.gov/news/world-just-sweltered-through-its-hottest-august-on-record#:~:text
=by%20the%20numbers-,August%202023,174%2Dyear%20global%20clim
ate%20record.

91. Meckler, "Heat Wave Is Shutting Schools."

92. Baltimore City Public Schools, "Schools Without Air Conditioning: Week of September 5," August 31, 2023, https://www.baltimorecityschools.org /schoolswithoutacplan.

93. R. Jisung Park, "Heat and Learning," *American Economic Journal: Economic Policy* 12, no. 2 (2020): 306–339.

94. Perry E. Sheffield, "Climate Change and Schools: Environmental Hazards and Resiliency," *International Journal of Environmental Research and Public Health* 14, no. 11 (2017), article 1397, https://doi.org/10.3390/ijerph14111397.

95. Sheffield, "Climate Change and Schools."

96. Centers for Disease Control and Prevention, *Youth Risk Behavior Survey: Data Summary & Trends Report*, 2021, https://www.cdc.gov/healthyyouth/data /yrbs/pdf/yrbs_data-summary-trends_report2023_508.pdf.

97. Centers for Disease Control and Prevention, *Youth Risk Behavior Survey*, 59.

98. Centers for Disease Control and Prevention, *Youth Risk Behavior Survey*.

99. American Academy of Pediatrics, "AAP, AACAP, CHA Declare National Emergency in Children's Mental Health," *AAP News*, October 19, 2021, https:// publications.aap.org/aapnews/news/17718/AAP-AACAP-CHA-declare-nation al-emergency-in?autologincheck=redirected.

100. Sherry Everett Jones et al., "Family Economics and Mental Health Among High-School Students During COVID-19," *American Journal of Preventive Medicine* 64, no. 3 (2023): 416.

101. American Academy of Pediatrics, "AAP, AACAP, CHA Declare."

102. Libby Stanford, "Educators' Mental Health Gets New Attention in Federal Bill," *Education Week*, February 9, 2023, https://www.edweek.org/policy -politics/educators-mental-health-gets-new-attention-in-federal-bill/2023/02.

103. Greg J. Duncan and Jeanne Brooks-Gunn, eds., *Consequences of Growing Up Poor* (New York: Russell Sage Foundation, 1997).

104. Dave Davies, "Understanding the Mental Health Crisis Afflicting American Teens," *Fresh Air*, NPR, December 20, 2022, https://www.npr.org/2022/12 /20/1144354315/understanding-the-mental-health-crisis-afflicting-american -teens.

105. See, for example, Nicholas Zill and Charlotte A. Schoenborn, "Developmental, Learning, and Emotional Problems: Health of Our Nation's Children, United States, 1988," *Advance Data from Vital and Health Statistics*, no. 190 (1990): 1–18.

106. Jane D. McLeod and Michael J. Shanahan, "Trajectories of Poverty and Children's Mental Health," *Journal of Health and Social Behavior* 37, no. 3 (1996): 207–220.

107. Jones et al., "Family Economics and Mental Health."

108. Jones et al., "Family Economics and Mental Health."

109. Yunyu Xiao, "COVID-19 Policies, Pandemic Disruptions, and Changes in Child Mental Health and Sleep in the United States," *JAMA Network Open* 6, no. 3 (2023), article e232716, https://doi.org/10.1001/jamanetworkopen.2023.2716.

110. Ali Rowhani-Rahbar and Caitlin Moe, "School Shootings in the U.S.: What Is the State of Evidence?," *Journal of Adolescent Health* 64, no. 6 (2019): 683–684.

111. David Paradice, "An Analysis of US School Shooting Data (1840–2015)," *Education* 138, no. 2 (2017): 135–144.

112. John Woodrow Cox et al., "More Than 311,000 Students Have Experienced Gun Violence at School Since Columbine," *Washington Post*, September 2022, https://www.washingtonpost.com/graphics/2018/local/school-shootings-database/?utm_term1/4.8cb747ab6323.

113. Cox et al., "More Than 311,000 Students."

114. Áine Travers, Tracey McDonagh, and Ask Elklit, "Youth Responses to School Shootings: A Review," *Current Psychiatry Reports* 20 (2018): 1–9.

115. James Alan Fox and Emma E. Fridel, "The Menace of School Shootings in America: Panic and Overresponse," in *The Wiley Handbook on Violence in Education: Forms, Factors, and Preventions*, ed. H. Shapiro (New York: Wiley/Blackwell, 2018), 15.

116. Stacy L. Butkus, "Investigating School Shootings from 1996 to 2019 for Processes Needed to Prevent and Respond to Future School Shootings: A Case Study" (EdD diss., Northcentral University, 2020), ProQuest 27829484.

117. Lauren Musu et al., *Indicators of School Crime and Safety: 2018* (NCES 2019-047/NCJ 252571), National Center for Education Statistics, https://files.eric.ed.gov/fulltext/ED594245.pdf.

118. Marika Waselewski, Blaire Alma Patterson, and Tammy Chang, "Active Shooter Drills in the United States: A National Study of Youth Experiences and Perceptions," *Journal of Adolescent Health* 67, no. 4 (2020): 509–513; Lauren Rygg, "School Shooting Simulations: At What Point Does Preparation Become More Harmful Than Helpful?," *Children's Legal Rights Journal* 35 (2015): 215–228.

119. Yunsoo Park, "When Students Don't Feel Safe in the Neighborhood: How Can Schools Help?," D.C. Policy Center, March 3, 2020, https://www.dcpolicycenter.org/publications/mental-health-supports/.

120. Rachel Martin et al., "Racial Disparities in Child Exposure to Firearm Violence Before and During COVID-19," *American Journal of Preventive Medicine* 63, no. 2 (2022): 204–212.

121. Tia M. McGill et al., "Effects of Exposure to Community Violence and Family Violence on School Functioning Problems Among Urban Youth: The Potential Mediating Role of Posttraumatic Stress Symptoms," *Frontiers in Public Health* 2 (2014): article 8, https://doi.org/10.3389/fpubh.2014.00008.

122. Samantha K. Stanley et al., "From Anger to Action: Differential Impacts of Eco-Anxiety, Eco-Depression, and Eco-Anger on Climate Action and Wellbeing,"

*Journal of Climate Change and Health* 1 (2021), article 100003, https://doi.org /10.1016/j.joclim.2021.100003.

123. Sarah E. O. Schwartz et al., "Climate Change Anxiety and Mental Health: Environmental Activism as Buffer," *Current Psychology* 42 (2023): 16709.

124. Caroline Preston, "Climate Change Is Sabotaging Education for America's Students—and It's Only Going to Get Worse," *Hechinger Report*, September 19, 2021, https://hechingerreport.org/climate-change-is-sabotaging-education -for-americas-students-and-its-only-going-to-get-worse/.

125. Caroline Preston, "Teaching Among the Ashes: "It's Not Just Your House That Burned. It's Everyone's," *Hechinger Report*, May 23, 2020, https://hechinger report.org/teaching-among-the-ashes-its-not-just-your-house-that-burned-its -everyones/.

126. Preston, "Climate Change."

127. Preston, "Climate Change."

128. Victoria Rideout and Michael B. Robb, *Social Media, Social Life: Teens Reveal Their Experiences*, Common Sense Media, 2018, https://www.common sensemedia.org/sites/default/files/research/report/2018-social-media-social -life-executive-summary-web.pdf.

129. Victoria Rideout, Alanna Peebles, and Micheal B. Robb, *Common Sense Census: Media Use by Tweens and Teens, 2021*, Common Sense, 2022, https://www .commonsensemedia.org/sites/default/files/research/report/8-18-census -integrated-report-final-web_0.pdf.

130. Elia Abi-Jaoude, Karline Treurnicht Naylor, and Antonio Pignatiello, "Smartphones, Social Media Use and Youth Mental Health," *Canadian Medical Association Journal* 192, no. 6 (2020): e136–e141, https://doi.org/10.1503/cmaj.190434.

131. Abi-Jaoude, Treurnicht Naylor, and Pignatiello, "Smartphones, Social Media Use."

132. National Association of School Psychologists, "State Shortages Data Dashboard," 2021, https://www.nasponline.org/about-school-psychology/state-short ages-data-dashboard.

133. Stephen Noonoo, "The Mental Health Crisis Causing Teachers to Quit," *EdSurge*, May 2, 2022, https://www.edsurge.com/news/2022-05-02-the-mental -health-crisis-causing-teachers-to-quit.

134. Elizabeth D. Steiner and Ashley Woo, *Job-Related Stress Threatens the Teacher Supply: Key Findings from the 2021 State of the U.S. Teacher Survey*, RAND Corporation, 2021, https://www.rand.org/pubs/research_reports/RRA1108-1.html.

## CHAPTER 2

1. Linda Darling-Hammond, *The Flat World and Education: How America's Commitment to Equity Will Determine Our Future* (New York: Teachers College Press, 2010).

2. R. L'Heureux Lewis-McCoy, *Inequality in the Promised Land: Race, Resources, and Suburban Schooling* (Stanford, CA: Stanford University Press, 2014); David M.

Merolla, "Self-Efficacy and Academic Achievement: The Role of Neighborhood Cultural Context," *Sociological Perspectives* 60, no. 2 (2017): 378–393.

3. Sarah D. Sparks, "Title I Explained: 5 Things Educators Need to Understand About Federal Money for Students in Poverty," *Education Week*, May 9, 2019, http://blogs .edweek.org/edweek/inside-school-research/2019/05/understanding_how_title _i_grants_work.html.

4. Robert E. Slavin, "Comprehensive School Reform," in *21st Century Education: A Reference Handbook*, ed. Thomas L. Good (Los Angeles: Sage, 2007), 259–266.

5. Lisa Staresina, "Comprehensive School Reform," *Education Week*, September 10, 2004, https://www.edweek.org/leadership/comprehensive-school-reform /2004/09.

6. Robert E. Slavin, "Evidence-Based Education Policies: Transforming Educational Practice and Research," *Educational Researcher* 31, no. 7 (2002): 15–21.

7. Toni A. Sondergeld and Kristin L. K. Koskey, "Evaluating the Impact of an Urban Comprehensive School Reform: An Illustration of the Need for Mixed Methods," *Studies in Educational Evaluation* 37, nos. 2–3 (2011): 94–107.

8. Hal A. Lawson and Dolf van Veen, "A Shared Rationale for New School Designs with Place-Based Differences," in *Developing Community Schools, Community Learning Centers, Extended-Service Schools and Multi-Service Schools: International Exemplars for Practice, Policy and Research*, ed. Hal A. Lawson and Dolf van Veen (New York: Springer, 2016), 23–47.

9. Rebecca Winthrop, "Open Letter to the Incoming Biden Administration on Next Generation Community Schools," Brookings Institute, December 18, 2020, https://www.brookings.edu/blog/education-plus-development/2020 /12/18/open-letter-to-the-incoming-biden-administration-on-next-generation -community-schools/?preview_id=1307880.

10. US Department of Education, "U.S. Department of Education Announces $63 Million to Expand Community Schools and Increase Social, Emotional, Mental Health, and Academic Support for Students, Educators, and Families," press release, January 18, 2023, https://www.ed.gov/news/press-releases/us -department-education-announces-63-million-expand-community-schools -and-increase-social-emotional-mental-health-and-academic-support -students-educators-and-families.

11. Anna Maier and Adrian Rivera-Rodriguez, *State Strategies for Investing in Community Schools*, Learning Policy Institute, April 18, 2023, https://learning policyinstitute.org/product/state-strategies-investing-in-community-schools -report.

12. Joy Dryfoos, "Full-Service Community Schools: A Strategy—Not a Program," *New Directions for Youth Development* 107 (2005): 7–14.

13. Anna Maier et al., *Community Schools as an Effective School Improvement Strategy: A Review of the Evidence*, Learning Policy Institute, 2017, https://

learningpolicyinstitute.org/media/137/download?inline&file=Community
_Schools_Effective_REPORT.pdf.

14. US Department of Education, "General Community School Resources," 2023,
https://oese.ed.gov/offices/office-of-discretionary-grants-support-services/sc
hool-choice-improvement-programs/full-service-community-schools-program
-fscs/general-resources/.

15. Jeannie Oakes et al., *Community Schools: An Evidence-Based Strategy for
Equitable School Improvement*, Learning Policy Institute, June 2017, https://
learningpolicyinstitute.org/product/community-schools-equitable
-improvement-brief.

16. Vanessa Sacks et al., "Integrated Student Supports in Schools May Boost
Lifetime Incomes for Students in Families with Low Incomes," Child Trends,
December 15, 2022, https://www.childtrends.org/publications/integrated
-student-supports-in-schools-may-boost-lifetime-incomes-for-students-in-fam
ilies-with-low-incomes.

17. US Department of Education, "Promise Neighborhoods: Cradle to Career,"
2021, accessed December 15, 2021, https://promiseneighborhoods.ed.gov/.

18. Stephanie M. Jones, and Emily J. Doolittle, "Social and Emotional Learning:
Introducing the Issue," *The Future of Children* 27, no. (2017): 3–11.

19. Linda Darling-Hammond et al., *Restarting and Reinventing School: Learning in
the Time of COVID and Beyond*, Learning Policy Institute, August 2020, https://
files.eric.ed.gov/fulltext/ED610890.pdf.

20. Association for Supervision and Curriculum Development, "The ASCD Whole
Child Approach to Education," 2023, https://www.ascd.org/whole-child.

21. Abraham Maslow and K. J. Lewis, "Maslow's Hierarchy of Needs," *Salenger
Incorporated* 14, no. 17 (1987): 987–990.

22. Avneet Kaur, "Maslow's Need Hierarchy Theory: Applications and Criti-
cisms," *Global Journal of Management and Business Studies* 3, no. 10 (2013):
1061–1064.

23. Rodwan Hashim Mohammed Fallatah and Jawad Syed, *Employee Motivation in
Saudi Arabia: An Investigation into the Higher Education Sector* (Cham, Switzer-
land: Palgrave Macmillan, 2018), 19–59.

24. Benjamin F. Henwood et al., "Maslow and Mental Health Recovery: A Comparative Study of Homeless Programs for Adults with Serious Mental Illness,"
*Administration and Policy in Mental Health and Mental Health Services Research*
42 (2015): 220–228.

25. Sophie King-Hill, "Critical Analysis of Maslow's Hierarchy of Need," *STeP Journal (Student Teacher Perspectives)* 2, no. 4 (2015): 54–57.

26. Mary E. Walsh and Claire Foley, *City Connects: Intervention & Impact Progress Report
2020*, Boston College, Center for Optimized Student Support, 2020, https://www
.bc.edu/content/dam/bc1/schools/lsoe/centers/city-connects/coss/City%20
Connects%20progress%20report%202020.pdf, p. 6. Emphasis added.

27. Dan W. Rea and Cordelia D. Zinskie, "Educating Students in Poverty: Building Equity and Capacity with a Holistic Framework and Community School Model," *National Youth Advocacy and Resilience Journal* 2, no. 2 (2017): 1–24.

28. Michael A. Gottfried, "Excused Versus Unexcused: How Student Absences in Elementary School Affect Academic Achievement," *Educational Evaluation and Policy Analysis* 31, no. 4 (2009): 392–415.

29. Mayumi A. Willgerodt, Douglas M. Brock, and Erin D. Maughan, "Public School Nursing Practice in the United States," *Journal of School Nursing* 34, no. 3 (2018): 232–244.

30. Christine Vestal, "School Nurse Deficit Deepens as States Seek Relief," *Stateline*, October 26, 2021, https://www.pewtrusts.org/en/research-and-analysis/blogs/stateline/2021/10/26/school-nurse-deficit-deepens-as-states-seek-relief.

31. Elizabeth Hinkson et al., "Medication Administration in Schools: (Position Statement)," National Association of School Nurses, 2017, https://files.eric.ed.gov/fulltext/ED581613.pdf.

32. Elaine Weiss and Paul Reville, *Broader, Bolder, Better: How Schools and Communities Help Students Overcome the Disadvantages of Poverty* (Cambridge, MA: Harvard Education Press, 2019).

33. Tim Walker, "Are Schools Ready to Tackle the Mental Health Crisis?," *NEA Today*, September 13, 2018, https://www.nea.org/advocating-for-change/new-from-nea/are-schools-ready-tackle-mental-health-crisis.

34. Jal Mehta and Sarah Fine, *In Search of Deeper Learning: The Quest to Remake the American High School* (Cambridge, MA: Harvard University Press, 2019).

35. Kaisa Snellman, Jennifer M. Silva, and Robert D. Putnam, "Inequity Outside the Classroom: Growing Class Differences in Participation in Extracurricular Activities," *Voices in Urban Education*, no. 40 (2015): 7–14, https://files.eric.ed.gov/fulltext/EJ1056739.pdf.

36. Anne Henderson and Nancy Berla, eds., *A New Generation of Evidence: The Family Is Critical to Student Achievement*, National Committee for Citizens in Education, 1994, https://files.eric.ed.gov/fulltext/ED375968.pdf.

37. Anne Henderson and Karen L. Mapp, *A New Wave of Evidence: The Impact of School, Family, and Community Connections on Student Achievement*, Southwest Educational Development Laboratory, 2002, https://files.eric.ed.gov/fulltext/ED474521.pdf.

38. Catherine Jacques and Alma Villegas, *Strategies for Equitable Family Engagement*, State Support Network, December 2018, https://oese.ed.gov/files/2020/10/equitable_family_engag_508.pdf.

39. Ann M. Ishimaru, *Just Schools: Building Equitable Collaborations with Families and Communities* (New York: Teachers College Press, 2019).

40. In Vancouver, Washington, for example, Latinx parents, whose children comprised a growing share of the student body but who had historically been marginalized, expressed gratitude as schools welcomed not only their engagement,

but elevated them into leadership roles, helping them bring their peers into the district's FSCS schools to provide Spanish and cooking lessons, and other enrichment. See Weiss and Reville, *Broader, Bolder, Better*.

41. Andrea Mraz Esposito et al., "Promise Neighborhood Site Profile: Los Angeles Promise Neighborhood," Mathematica Policy Research, 2015, https://www.mathematica.org/publications/promise-neighborhood-site-profile-los-angeles-promise-neighborhood.

42. This support may come directly from the Coalition and/or its parent institution, IEL, from Coalition members such as the National Center for Community Schools, or from research institutions like universities or the Learning Policy Institute.

43. Weiss and Reville, *Broader, Bolder, Better*.

44. US Department of Education, "U.S. Department of Education."

45. White House, *White House Toolkit: Federal Resources to Support Community Schools*, January 13, 2023, https://www.whitehouse.gov/wp-content/uploads/2023/01/2023-01-13-WHITE-HOUSE-TOOLKIT_Federal-Resources-to-Support-Community-Schools.pdf.

46. Jill Biden, "Remarks as Prepared for Delivery by First Lady Jill Biden at the Communities in Schools (CIS) Leadership Town Hall Conference," White House, Washington, DC, October 19, 2022, https://www.whitehouse.gov/briefing-room/speeches-remarks/2022/10/19/remarks-as-prepared-for-delivery-by-first-lady-jill-biden-at-the-communities-in-schools-cis-leadership-town-hall-conference.

47. Coalition for Community Schools, "About: How We Do It," 2020, https://www.communityschools.org/about/who-we-are/.

48. Hayin Kimner, "Moving Community Schools Forward with Foundational Resources," Brookings Institute, January 12, 2023, https://www.brookings.edu/articles/moving-community-schools-forward-with-foundational-resources/.

49. Jeannie Oakes, Emily Germain, and Anna Maier, "Outcomes and Indicators for Community Schools: A Guide for Implementers and Evaluators," Community Schools Forward Series Learning Policy Institute, 2023, https://learningpolicyinstitute.org/media/3937/download?inline&file=CSF_Outcomes_Indicators_Community_Schools.pdf, p. 9.

50. Two of these communities—Berea and Minneapolis—were studied and featured in Weiss and Reville, *Broader, Bolder, Better*, while others—including Frederick County, Grain Valley, and Salem—were familiar to the authors but not a focus of that book.

51. US Department of Education, "Promise Neighborhoods."

## CHAPTER 3

1. Centers for Disease Control and Prevention, "1918 Pandemic (H1N1 Virus)," archived September 1, 2023, https://archive.cdc.gov/#/details?url=https://www.cdc.gov/flu/pandemic-resources/1918-pandemic-h1n1.html.

2. Nirmita Panchal, Cynthia Cox, and Robin Rudowitz, "The Landscape of School-Based Mental Health Services," Kaiser Family Foundation, September 6, 2022, https://www.kff.org/mental-health/issue-brief/the-landscape-of-school-based-mental-health-services/.

3. Maryland Out of School Time Network and the Maryland Coalition for Community Schools, *The CPG Toolkit: Implementing the Concentration of Poverty Provision of the Blueprint for Maryland's Future*, 2021, https://www.mostnetwork.org/wp-content/uploads/CGP-Updated.pdf, p. 13.

4. While the Fairbanks North Star Borough School District is not among the districts we worked with for this project, it is among several other Bright Futures affiliates that we collaborated with on other work of ours, jointly with former Joplin, Missouri, superintendent and Bright Futures USA founder C. J. Huff, in the year leading up to the pandemic and the first year in which schools were closed down. The insights gleaned with respect to its responses to COVID-19 were relevant and sufficiently noteworthy to include here. See Elaine Weiss and Paul Reville, *Broader, Bolder, Better: How Schools and Communities Help Students Overcome the Disadvantages of Poverty* (Cambridge, MA: Harvard Education Press, 2021).

5. Home visits have long been a core strategy employed by community schools. On October 24, 2023, for example, the Institute for Educational Leadership, which houses the Coalition for Community Schools, hosted a webinar on the subject in partnership with Welcoming America. See Welcoming America, "How Education Institutions and Community-Based Organizations Use Home Visits to Strengthen Connections with Newcomer and Immigrant Families," last modified October 27, 2023, https://welcomingamerica.org/resource/how-education-institutions-and-community-based-organizations-use-home-visits-to-strengthen-connections-with-newcomer-and-immigrant-families/.

6. Based out of Berea College, Kentucky, Partners for Education was relaunched in 2022 as Partners for Rural Impact, an independent nonprofit entity with its own space and structure. As our interviews with members of this organization took place in 2021, we use its name at that time, Partners for Education, when quoting those interviews, and when referring to events that occurred before the name change.

7. Kim Doleatto, "A Bus That Turns into a Preschool Classroom," The Patterson Foundation, February 21, 2020, https://www.thepattersonfoundation.org/blog/a-bus-that-turns-into-a-preschool-classroom.html.

8. Elaine Weiss and Paul Reville, *Broader, Bolder, Better: How Schools and Communities Help Students Overcome the Disadvantages of Poverty* (Cambridge, MA: Harvard Education Press, 2021).

9. As part of the intentional and systematic work to break intergenerational cycles of poverty and the impacts of structural racism, NAZ refers to their students as "scholars," a cultural premise that is meaningfully evident in the

conversation we had with every interviewee, from CEO Sondra Samuels to principal, teacher, and family achievement coach.

10. Sondra Samuels, CEO of NAZ, interview with authors, April 7, 2023.
11. Tatika Taylor, NAZ Family Achievement Coach, interview with authors, May 26, 2023.
12. Angelina Courtney, NAZ parent, interview with authors, June 21, 2023.
13. Dreama Gentry, CEO of Partners for Education, interview with authors, October 6, 2021.
14. Travis Mitchell, Sergeant, Frederick County Sheriff's Office, interview with authors, February 7, 2023.
15. Zoom was one of the most popular and widely used video conferencing tools used during the COVID-19 pandemic starting in 2020.
16. Athena Deaton, middle school science teacher in Berea, KY, interview with authors, January 25, 2023.
17. Deaton, interview with authors.
18. Katie LaGrone, "Thousands of Florida Students Still Reported 'Missing' from School Districts," *ABC Action News Tampa Bay*, October 6, 2021, https://www.abcactionnews.com/news/state/thousands-of-florida-students-still-reported-missing-from-school-districts.
19. Mia Riccio, Coordinator for City Connects in Salem, MA, interview with authors, February 2, 2023.
20. See, for example, Amy Joyce and Mari-Jane Williams, "Parenting During Coronavirus: What to Know About Play Dates, Online Learning, and More," *Washington Post*, March 25, 2020, https://www.washingtonpost.com/lifestyle/2020/03/14/parenting-tips-coronavirus/.
21. Deaton, interview with authors.
22. Riccio, interview with authors.
23. Charity Lezama, Executive Director of the YMCA of the North Shore, Salem, MA, interview with authors, February 16, 2023.
24. Riccio, interview with authors.
25. Ellen Wingard, Executive Director of Student and Family Support Services at Salem Public Schools, interview with authors, October 29, 2021.
26. Suzanne Miller, teacher at Frederick Middle School, interview with authors, November 11, 2021.
27. Nathan Perry, middle school history teacher at North Middle School in Grain Valley, MO, interview with authors, February 7, 2023.
28. Perry, interview with authors.
29. Deaton, interview with authors.
30. Mitchell, interview with authors.
31. Paula Johannsen, Parent Liaison, Bright Futures at Millbrook High School in Frederick County, VA, interview with authors, November 12, 2021.

32. Amon Couch, Director of Programs for Partners for Education, interview with authors, July 8, 2021.
33. Deaton, interview with authors.
34. Beth Dotson Brown, Project Director at Partners for Education, interview with authors, July 8, 2021.
35. Gentry, interview with authors.
36. Lezama, interview with authors.
37. Katie Reilly, "How Schools Are Working to Help Kids Recover from Pandemic Learning Loss," Time, August 25, 2022, https://time.com/6208737/tutoring -pandemic-learning-loss-tennessee/.
38. "Medically fragile" and other students whose parents felt strongly could petition to stay home, but the district developed clear limits in an effort to bring as many students into classrooms in person as possible.
39. David T. Sovine, EdD, Superintendent of Frederick County Public Schools, interview with authors, June 29, 2021.
40. Nancy Mango, Program Coordinator, Bright Futures Frederick/Winchester, interview with authors, November 8, 2021.
41. Sovine, interview with authors.
42. For more information, see https://www.chfs.ky.gov/agencies/dfrcvs/dfrysc /Pages/default.aspx.
43. Deaton, interview with authors.
44. Samuels, interview with authors.
45. Samuels, interview with authors.
46. Lezama, interview with authors.
47. Gentry, interview with authors.
48. Perry, interview with authors.
49. Perry, interview with authors.
50. Jenny Hobson, Family and Community Engagement Specialist at Partners for Education, interview with authors, December 14, 2021.
51. Deaton, interview with authors.
52. Wingard, interview with authors.
53. Riccio, interview with authors.
54. In March 2023, McKenzie became Family Friendly Schools Director for the Prichard Committee.
55. Grace McKenzie, Associate Director of Family Partnerships with Partners for Education, interview with authors, October 15, 2021.
56. Perry, interview with authors.
57. Miller, interview with authors.
58. Lezama, interview with authors.
59. Wingard, interview with authors.
60. C. J. Huff, EdD, Education Consultant and Disaster Recovery Expert, correspondence with authors.

61. National Center for Education Statistics, "Roughly Half of Public Schools Report That They Can Effectively Provide Mental Health Services to All Students in Need," press release,, May 3, 2022, https://nces.ed.gov/whatsnew /press_releases/05_31_2022_2.asp.

62. Jocelyn Gecker and Dylan Lovan, "Youth Mental Health Is in Crisis. Are Schools Doing Enough?," Associated Press, August 17, 2022, https://apnews.com/article /mental-health-crisis-schools-768fed6a4e71d694ec0694c627d8fdca.

63. Marisa Charpentier, "Thousands of Central Texans Are Facing Hunger Because of the Pandemic: The Need Isn't Going Away Anytime Soon," Kut News, December 17, 2020, https://www.kut.org/covid-19/2020-12-17/thousands-of-central -texans-are-facing-hunger-because-of-the-pandemic-the-need-isnt-going-away -any-time-soon; Katie LaGrone, "Thousands of Florida Students Still Reported 'Missing' from School Districts," ABC Action News Tampa Bay, October 6, 2021, https://www.abcactionnews.com/news/state/thousands-of-florida-students -still-reported-missing-from-school-districts.

## CHAPTER 4

1. Ronald Lindahl, "Shared Leadership: Can It Work in Schools?," *Educational Forum* 72, no. 4 (2008): 298–307.

2. See Donna Braun et al., "Improving Equitable Student Outcomes: A Transformational and Collaborative Leadership Development Approach," *Journal of Educational Leadership and Policy Studies* 5, no. 1 (2021): 1–24.

3. Anthony Bryk et al., *Organizing Schools for Improvement: Lessons from Chicago* (Chicago: University of Chicago Press, 2010).

4. Anna Maier, Jeannie Oakes, and Tiffany Miller, "Community Schools," Learning Policy Institute, https://learningpolicyinstitute.org/topic/community -schools. Emphasis added.

5. Athena Deaton, Middle School Science Teacher, Berea, KY, interview with authors, January 25, 2023.

6. Deaton, interview with authors.

7. Sondra Samuels, CEO of the Northside Achievement Zone, interview with authors, April 7, 2023.

8. Samuels, interview with authors.

9. Nathan Perry, History Teacher at Grain Valley North Middle School, MO, interview with authors, February 7, 2023.

10. Ellen Wingard, Executive Director of Student and Family Support Services at Salem Public Schools, interview with authors, October 29, 2021.

11. Mia Riccio, City Connects Coordinator, Salem, MA, interview with authors, February 2, 2023.

12. Robyn Burns, Executive Director at the Salem Pantry, interview with authors, February 2, 2023.

13. Charity Lezama, Executive Director at the YMCA of the North Shore, Salem, MA, interview with authors, February 16, 2023.
14. Perry, interview with authors.
15. Perry, interview with authors.
16. Paula Johannsen, Bright Futures Parent Liaison at Millbrook High School, Frederick County, VA, interview with authors, November 12, 2021.
17. Wingard, interview with authors.
18. Riccio, interview with authors.
19. Perry, interview with authors.
20. Kelly Schick, School Counselor at Grain Valley North Middle School, MO, interview with authors, January 27, 2023.
21. Samuels, interview with authors.
22. Deaton, interview with authors.
23. Deaton, interview with authors.
24. Deaton, interview with authors.
25. Deaton, interview with authors.
26. Shontya' Washington, School Board member and parent, Frederick County Public Schools, VA, interview with authors, November 9, 2021.
27. Washington, interview with authors.
28. Wingard, interview with authors.

CHAPTER 5

1. Dreama Gentry, Executive Director of Partners for Education (PFE), interview with authors, October 6, 2021.
2. Gentry, interview with authors.
3. Partners for Rural Impact (PRI), "Berea College's Newest Graduate Is . . . a Nonprofit?," November 2023, https://partnersrural.org/wp-content/uploads/2022/07/PRI-Launch-long-version.pdf. Emphasis added.
4. PRI has since received additional grants, enabling it to expand its Full-service Community School supports to over a hundred schools across Eastern Kentucky.
5. Brookings Institution, "Essential Resources for Driving Community Schools Forward," January 12, 2023, https://www.brookings.edu/events/essential-resources-for-driving-community-schools-forward/.
6. J. Morgan, associate vice president of strategic communications at PRI, email correspondence with Elaine Weiss, August 2023.
7. J. Morgan, associate vice president of strategic communications at PRI, email correspondence with Elaine Weiss, August 2023.
8. PRI's Appalachian Cradle to Career Partnership is designed "to achieve equitable life outcomes for all youth and children in the eight-county southeastern Kentucky Promise Zone, [with] five regional nonprofits aligned to create a cross-sector backbone partnership." PRI, "Our Model," accessed March 1, 2024, https://partnersrural.org/our-work/.

9. Northside Achievement Zone (NAZ), *FY22–FY24 Strategic Plan: Going Deeper, Going Wider,* December 2021, https://www.northsideachievement.org/sites /default/files/2023-04/Strategic-Business-Plan-December-2021.pdf.

10. Sondra Samuels, CEO of NAZ, interview with authors, April 7, 2023.

11. Angelina Courtney, NAZ parent, interview with authors, June 21, 2023.

12. Tatika Taylor, NAZ Family Achievement Coach, interview with authors, May 26, 2023.

13. Samuels, interview with authors.

14. Samuels, interview with authors.

15. Benito Matias, Principal of Ascension Catholic School, interview with authors, May 12, 2023.

16. Mia Riccio, City Connects Coordinator, Salem, MA, interview with authors, February 2, 2023.

17. Talewise, Homepage, 2023, https://www.talewise.com/.

18. Ellen Wingard, Executive Director of Student and Family Support Services at Salem Public Schools, interview with authors, October 29, 2021.

19. Mario Giamporcaro, Guidance Counselor at Frederick County Middle School, VA, interview with authors, November 22, 2021.

20. Giamporcaro, interview with authors.

21. Frederick County Public Schools, *Inspire 2025: A Promise for Progress,* https:// www.frederickcountyschoolsva.net/cms/lib/VA50000684/Centricity /Domain/140/inspire_2025_strategic_plan_102219.pdf.

22. Nathan Perry, History Teacher at Grain Valley North Middle School, MO, interview with authors, February 7, 2023.

23. Dale Smith, PhD, Senior Pastor at Road Church in Grain Valley, MO, interview with authors, March 14, 2023.

24. Gentry, interview with authors.

25. Perry, interview with authors.

26. Kelly Schick, School Counselor at Grain Valley North Middle School, MO, interview with authors, January 27, 2023.

27. Matias, interview with authors.

28. As the investigation into the Parkland, Florida, school shooting demonstrates, school resource officers (SROs) may not prevent massacres. Moreover, a growing body of evidence suggests that SROs contribute to the many students' anxiety and challenges related to the "school to prison pipeline." See Christina Pigott, Ami E. Stearns, and David N. Khey, "School Resource Officers and the School to Prison Pipeline: Discovering Trends of Expulsions in Public Schools," *American Journal of Criminal Justice* 43 (2018): 120–138.

29. Travis Mitchell, Sergeant, Frederick County Sheriff's Office, interview with authors, February 7, 2023.

30. Mitchell, interview with authors.

31. Mitchell, interview with authors.

32. Courtney, interview with authors.
33. Courtney, interview with authors.
34. Courtney, interview with authors.

## CHAPTER 6

1. Sylvia Allegretto, Emma Garcia, and Elaine Weiss, *Public Education Funding in the U.S. Needs an Overhaul: How a Larger Federal Role Would Boost Equity and Shield Children from Disinvestment During Downturns*, Economic Policy Institute, July 12, 2022, https://files.epi.org/uploads/233143.pdf.
2. Allegretto, Garcia, and Weiss, *Public Education Funding*, 30 and n.21. The percentage comes from Allegretto's analysis of Bureau of Labor Statistics Current Employment Statistics data for 2019.
3. Allegretto, Garcia, and Weiss, *Public Education Funding*, 30–31.
4. Jennifer S. Vey and Juanita Morales, "Why Local Leaders Should Champion Community Schools to Improve Student, Family, and Neighborhood Well-Being," Brookings Institution, December 12, 2022, https://www.brookings.edu/articles/why-local-leaders-should-champion-community-schools-to-improve-student-family-and-neighborhood-well-being/.
5. Laura Martinez and Cheryl D. Hayes, "Measuring Social Return on Investment for Community Schools: A Case Study," The Finance Project and The Children's Aid Society (2013). https://files.eric.ed.gov/fulltext/ED561996.pdf.
6. Sonny S. Patel et al., "What Do We Mean by 'Community Resilience'? A Systematic Literature Review of How It Is Defined in the Literature," *PLoS Currents* 9 (2017), https://www.ncbi.nlm.nih.gov/pmc/articles/PMC5693357/.
7. Patel et al., "What Do We Mean?"
8. Cindy Long, "Public Schools Offer Shelter from the Storm," *NEA News*, September 15, 2017, https://www.nea.org/nea-today/all-news-articles/public-schools-offer-shelter-storm.
9. Kenzo Takahashi et al., "School Health: An Essential Strategy in Promoting Community Resilience and Preparedness for Natural Disasters," *Global Health Action* 8, no. 1 (2015), article 29106.
10. Jacob Fay et al., "Schools During the COVID-19 Pandemic: Sites and Sources of Community Resilience," Edmond J. Safra Center for Ethics, White Paper 20, June 11, 2020, 2, https://jhdimpact.org/wp-content/uploads/2023/01/20schoolsduringpandemic2.pdf.
11. Robyn Burns, Executive Director of the Salem Pantry, interview with authors, February 2, 2023.
12. Nancy Mango, Bright Futures Program Coordinator, interview with authors, November 8, 2021.
13. Jiying Ling, Paige Duren, and Lorraine B. Robbins, "Food Insecurity and Mental Well-Being Among Low-Income Families During COVID-19 Pandemic," *American Journal of Health Promotion* 36, no. 7 (2022): 1123–1132; Food Research

and Action Center, "Benefits of School Lunch," 2023, https://frac.org/programs
/national-school-lunch-program/benefits-school-lunch.

14. Michael J. Lawler et al., "Ecological, Relationship-Based Model of Children's
Subjective Well-Being: Perspectives of 10-Year-Old Children in the United
States and 10 Other Countries," *Child Indicators Research* 10 (2017): 1–18.

15. Ellen Wingard, Executive Director of Student and Family Support Services at
Salem Public Schools, interview with authors, October 29, 2021.

16. Robert E. Drake and Gary R. Bond, "Psychiatric Crisis Care and the More Is Less
Paradox," *Community Mental Health Journal* 57, no. 7 (2021): 1230–1236.

17. Sondra Samuels, CEO of the Northside Achievement Zone, interview with
authors, April 7, 2023.

18. Travis Mitchell, Sergeant, Frederick County Sheriff's Office, interview with
authors, February 7, 2023.

19. Jennifer P. Edidin et al., "The Mental and Physical Health of Homeless Youth: A
Literature Review," *Child Psychiatry & Human Development* 43 (2012): 354–375.

20. Peter M. Miller, "A Critical Analysis of the Research on Student Homelessness,"
*Review of Educational Research* 81, no. 3 (2011): 308–337.

21. Elaine Weiss and Paul Reville, *Broader, Bolder, Better: How Schools and Communities Help Students Overcome the Disadvantages of Poverty* (Cambridge, MA: Harvard Education Press, 2021).

22. Bright Futures USA, "Our Story: A Bright Idea," 2022, https://brightfuturesusa
.org/our-story/.

## CHAPTER 7

1. Joe Pinsker, "Parental Leave Is American Exceptionalism at Its Bleakest," *Atlantic*, November 9, 2021, https://www.theatlantic.com/family/archive/2021/11
/us-paid-family-parental-leave-congress-bill/620660/; National Council on
Aging, "Addressing the Nation's Retirement Crisis: The 80%," April 10, 2023,
https://www.ncoa.org/article/addressing-the-nations-retirement-crisis-the
-80-percent-financially-struggling.

2. Southern Education Foundation, "A New Majority: Low Income Students in
the South and Nation," October 2013, https://southerneducation.org/wp
-content/uploads/documents/new-majority-2013.pdf.

3. Jessica Lapham and Melissa L. Martinson, "The Intersection of Welfare Stigma,
State Contexts and Health Among Mothers Receiving Public Assistance Benefits," *SSM-Population Health* 18 (2022), article 101117.

4. Katherine Lanca et al., "Universal School Meals Increased Student Participation, Reduced Stigma," *Food Blog* [University of California Division of Agriculture and Natural Resources], March 14, 2023, https://ucanr.edu/blogs/blogcore
/postdetail.cfm?postnum=56451.

5. David T. Sovine, EdD, Superintendent, Frederick County Public Schools, interview with authors, June 29, 2021.; The acronym SMART was first proposed by

George T. Doran in "There's a S.M.A.R.T. Way to Write Management's Goals and Objectives," *Management Review* 70, no. 11: 35–36. Doran recommends setting objectives that are Specific, Measurable, Assignable, Realistic, and Time-bound (SMART).

6. Joshua Becker, "61% of Americans Live Paycheck-to-Paycheck: Here's the Simple Solution We're Overlooking," *Forbes*, August 18, 2023, https://www.forbes.com /sites/joshuabecker/2023/08/18/61-of-americans-live-paycheck-to-paycheck -heres-the-simple-solution-were-overlooking/?sh=697b2952c768.

7. Sylvia Allegretto, Emma Garcia, and Elaine Weiss, *Public Education Funding in the U.S. Needs an Overhaul; How a Larger Federal Role Would Boost Equity and Shield Children from Disinvestment During Downturns*, Economic Policy Institute, July 12, 2022. https://www.epi.org/publication/public-education-funding-in -the-us-needs-an-overhaul.

8. Michael Titus, Principal of Collins Middle School, Salem, MA, interview with authors, February 21, 2023.

9. Benito Matias, Principal of Ascension Catholic School, North Minneapolis, MN, interview with authors, May 12, 2023.

10. Athena Deaton, Middle School Science Teacher in Berea, KY, interview with authors, January 25, 2023.

11. Tim Pressley, "Factors Contributing to Teacher Burnout During COVID-19," *Educational Researcher* 50, no. 5 (2021): 325–327.

12. Grace McKenzie, Associate Director of Family Partnership for Partners for Education (PFE), interview with authors, October 15, 2021.

13. McKenzie, interview with authors.

14. Rav Arora, "A New Anti-Police Proposal in Minneapolis Would Endanger Black Lives," *New York Post*, October 2, 2021, https://nypost.com/2021/10/02/a -minneapolis-anti-police-proposal-would-endanger-black-lives/.

15. Jack Healy and Nicholas Bogel-Burroughs, "Calls for Transforming Police Run into Realities of Governing in Minnesota," *New York Times*, June 12, 2020, https:// www.nytimes.com/2020/06/12/us/minneapolis-police-defunding.html.

16. Sondra Samuels, CEO of Northside Achievement Zone (NAZ), interview with authors, April 7, 2023.

17. Tatika Taylor, NAZ Family Achievement Coach, interview with authors, May 26, 2023.

18. Samuels, interview with authors.

19. Samuels, interview with authors.

20. Matias, interview with authors.

21. Dreama Gentry, Executive Director of PFE, interview with authors, October 6, 2021.

# ACKNOWLEDGMENTS

THE AUTHORS ARE GRATEFUL to every educator, school and district staff member, official, volunteer, parent, and family member who took the time to speak with us over the past few years. We have learned a tremendous amount, and you have inspired us at a time when we all could use inspiration. We hope that this book does justice to your excellent hard work and dedication to making your communities' schools safe, supportive, nurturing learning environments for every child. We appreciate the many researchers across a range of fields whose work laid the foundation for and informed this book in various ways. We also want to thank our editor, Shannon Davis, our development editor, Marisa Pagano, and all the Harvard Education Press staff for their guidance and support. You all made this book possible and better.

# ACKNOWLEDGMENTS

# ABOUT THE AUTHORS

**ELAINE WEISS** is an education policy analyst who has conducted research and led advocacy work at the National Academy of Social Insurance, Economic Policy Institute, and Pew Charitable Trusts. She is the coauthor, with Paul Reville, of *Broader, Bolder, Better: How Schools and Communities Help Students Overcome the Disadvantages of Poverty* (Harvard Education Press, 2019).

**BRUCE LEVINE** is a clinical professor and director of the Education Policy Program in Drexel University's School of Education. He is cofounder of the Community Schools Hub, an online project of that school, and is actively involved in other research initiatives examining the impact of schools providing integrated student supports.

**KIMBERLY STERIN** has worked as an educator, researcher, and policy analyst within and in partnership with public school districts, higher education institutions, and advocacy organizations. Her research interrogates the ways power is leveraged across the K–12 school finance and resource landscape with a focus on educational justice for historically marginalized groups.

# INDEX